With Best
Wishes
from Helen Kdy
Meh 5/1951

A PICTURE HISTORY OF CANADA

ST. GEORGE   ST. ANDREW   ST. PATRICK

UNION JACK   ROYAL STANDARD

RED ENSIGN   CANADA

A MARI VSQVE AD MARE

ARMS OF CANADA

THE UNION JACK AND THE FLAG AND ARMS
OF CANADA

A Picture History
of
Canada

By
Jessie McEwen and Kathleen Moore

Illustrated by Famous Artists

REVISED AND ENLARGED EDITION

THOMAS NELSON & SONS (CANADA) LIMITED

PRINTED IN GREAT BRITAIN BY
THOMAS NELSON AND SONS LTD
PARKSIDE WORKS EDINBURGH 9

Contents

Contents

List of Illustrations

Foreword

THE pages of our history are filled with so many exciting events that to attempt to tell Canada's story in only forty-eight pictures calls for a word of explanation.

When the artists and authors found themselves limited in choice they gave preference to incidents and events which contributed directly to the growth of Canada's nationhood. They intentionally chose, too, those subjects which illustrate most graphically the daily life of ordinary people. The two exceptions of Madeleine de Verchères and Laura Secord have the sanction of an almost sacred tradition.

Hackneyed subjects of illustration have been avoided. Instead of showing Lord Strathcona driving the last spike of the Canadian Pacific Railway, a new picture, specially painted by E. J. Dinsmore, illustrates the work of laying the bands of steel that brought " the east to the west, and the west to the east." Similarly a summertime crowd of men and women and young folks in front of the new Parliament Buildings in the early 'seventies has been chosen, because it is more typical of Canadian life of the period than the familiar group known as " The Fathers of Confederation."

Explorers and the part they played in our country's growth are honoured in these pages, but the authors regret that such names as Le Moyne d'Iberville, Samuel Hearne, and George Vancouver had to be left out. They would like to have had space to devote to such outstanding figures of statesmanship as Robert Baldwin, Joseph Howe, Sir James Douglas, Sir John A. MacDonald, George Brown, Sir Wilfrid Laurier, and many others. Despite these inevitable omissions, however, the story unfolded here gives a first glimpse of Canada's romantic story, and the authors feel that the purpose of the book will have been achieved if it gives to young readers a vivid background for a more detailed narrative of our country's history.

1. LIEF ERICSON SAILS INTO THE WEST

BIARNI, the traveller, made many journeys from Iceland to Norway, and when he returned from one of his voyages he learned that his father had gone to Greenland. Biarni had never been to Greenland, nor had he among his men any sailor who knew the waters near that land. Nevertheless he set out to find the land to which his father had gone. He sailed too far south and so missed Greenland, but after many days they saw a level land covered with woods. As Biarni did not think that this was Greenland, they pulled away from its shores and sailed northwards until they came to another shore.

" Neither can this be Greenland," Biarni said, " for Greenland has many great ice-mountains."

So again the men hoisted their sails, this time angrily, for they wanted to go ashore to get wood and drinking water. When they came to another land, this time high and mountainous, Biarni said, " Because this does not appear to offer any attractions, we shall sail on." As they left they saw that it was an island.

When at last they came to Greenland, and Biarni and his men told of the three lands they had seen, the people said he was foolish not to have explored the places that he had discovered.

At that time there was much talk of voyages of discovery, and when Lief, the son of Eric the Red, heard of the lands Biarni had seen, he resolved to explore them. Lief was a big, powerful man who was just in all things, and thirty-five men at once joined him. He bought a ship from Biarni, and they sailed out to sea. They came first to the land which Biarni had seen last. They went ashore; but when they saw that the land had no grass, but only flat rock and mountains, they left it.

They came next to a level land, and as they drew near it they saw that it had broad beaches of white sand. Lief named this land " Markland "; but as neither he nor his men liked it, they drew away from its shores and sailed south-westward.

THE VIKINGS DISCOVER AMERICA.
(*Fergus Kyle.*)

They came then to the land which Biarni had seen first, and when they went ashore they were greatly pleased. There was dew upon the grass, and when they tasted it they thought that never before had they tasted anything so sweet. The land delighted them so much that they decided to build themselves a house and to stay there for the winter. In the river and the lake which they discovered, they found salmon larger than any they had seen before.

" I propose now," Lief said to his men after their house had been built, " that we divide our company into two groups and set about an exploration of the country. One half of our company shall remain at home, and the other half shall investigate the land. . . . But those who go forth to search the land must return home each night."

Sometimes Lief led those who explored, and when he remained at home Tyrker, his foster-brother, led the expedition. Now one day Tyrker was missing when the men returned, and as he did not come to the house during the night Lief was sorely distressed. In the late afternoon of the next day, just as Lief was sending out a party of searchers, he appeared at the door with laughter in his eyes and eager words on his lips.

" See ! " he shouted. " See ! I have found vines and grapes. Do not doubt me, for I came from a land where there is no lack of either."

Tyrker had come to Greenland from the land of the Rhine, and he was able to show the Norsemen how to make wine from the rich fruits of the vines. When they returned to Greenland they filled their after-boat with grapes. They took salmon, and fine tall timbers for masts with them too, but it was from the grapes they named the land, for Lief called it " Vinland."

For many years afterward Vikings came to the land which Biarni had discovered and which Lief had explored. It was a land they loved dearly, and the tales which they told of it are written down in an old book which is now in the Royal Library at Copenhagen. From that old writing we know that the land of Lief was indeed part of our own continent of America.

2. COLUMBUS SEEKS THE INDIES

ABOUT five hundred years ago an Italian boy played with his brothers around the harbour of Genoa. They delighted in watching the sailing ships and galleys that brought merchandise from strange and distant lands. There were silks, camphor, and spices from India and Cathay, ivory from Africa, cloth, timber, and amber from the north of Europe. Genoa was then one of the busiest ports in the world, with ships coming and going every day, so it was natural that young Christopher Columbus soon decided to be a sailor.

No doubt it was this ambition which helped him at school to learn all about angles and circles, how to use the compass, and how to find one's way by the sun and stars. He meant to have a ship of his own some day, and would need to know these things in order to navigate it.

At fourteen he left school and sailed in his uncle's ship. His first voyages were not very long, but they were exciting, for Moorish pirates swarmed in the Mediterranean. Later on he sailed to Lisbon, where he met many other sailors, who told strange tales of seafaring. Some spoke of land sighted far over the western ocean, others told of picking up, far out at sea, pieces of wood curiously carved, and unlike anything seen in Europe.

Now at school Columbus had been taught that the world was round, although most people then believed it was flat. His talk with other sailors made him sure it was round, and he longed to have a ship of his own so that he could prove it. Besides, if it were round, one would sail to the Indies and Cathay more quickly by going west.

But Columbus was too poor to fit out a ship for himself, and for many years he failed to get any one to help him. He was forty-six years old, and his hair was grey, before he at last won the support of King Ferdinand and Queen Isabella of Spain.

COLUMBUS SETS SAIL
(From an old print.)

With three small ships and a doubting, fearful crew he set sail from Palos in August of the year 1492.

As the last streak of land disappeared below the horizon his crew became restless and anxious. They were accustomed to coastal sailing with land always in sight, and this was something very different. Besides, they believed the world was flat, and that therefore they might easily sail over the edge in the dark! But day and night Columbus held on westward with a favouring breeze.

In spite of his efforts to calm them the fears of his crew turned to anger, and as the days ran into weeks their anger turned to hatred. A mutiny was threatened, when something happened which made them think Columbus perhaps was right. A strange bird was sighted; then masses of seaweed and some drifting wood. Land *must* be near.

One night a light was seen in the west. It disappeared, and how eagerly every one scanned the horizon! At two o'clock in the morning the leading ship fired a gun—the signal of land in sight. By sunrise they could all see it, a green, tree-covered island.

Carrying the banner of Spain, Columbus landed and gave thanks to God for granting his heart's desire.

It was not, as he thought, an island of Asia, but San Salvador, in the West Indies, the outpost of a new continent. Much honour was paid him on returning to Spain, but many years passed before men realized the vastness of the New World.

3. CABOT AND THE "NEW FOUND LAND"

COLUMBUS was by no means the first or the only sailor who set out to find land across the Atlantic.

From ancient times western Europe had been haunted with legends of strange continents and islands that lay beyond the setting sun. There was the fabled continent of Atlantis, spoken of by old writers; the Irish had a tale of St. Brandon's Isle in the west; and in Iceland the descendants of the Vikings would re-tell, during the long winter evenings, the saga of Lief the Lucky. So it was a fairly common thing for sailors to search far out in the Atlantic for land of any sort.

The port of Bristol, in England, was then one of the great ports of Europe. It traded with Lisbon, Venice, and Genoa, and with Ireland, and sent ships even as far as Iceland. Columbus himself had visited the port of Bristol, and had made the Iceland voyage. Its merchants therefore took a keen interest in the discovery of new lands, and when the news came of the marvellous voyage of Columbus they were, of course, disappointed not to have had any share in it. The Bristol captains had been as diligent as any in the search of the western sea, and the merchants determined to make yet another effort, this time to try to find land north of that discovered by Columbus.

They chose as commander of the expedition John Cabot, a citizen of Venice, who took with him his three sons—Lewis, Sebastian, and Sanctus. The king (Henry VII.) granted them authority to take possession of any lands they might discover, which were unknown to Christian peoples. Cabot set sail in the spring of 1497, and his course took him near Iceland. He was following the track of Lief the Lucky, who had passed that way five hundred years before.

Little or nothing is known about the events of the voyage, or even what part of North America he discovered. It was either

CABOT EMBARKING
(Ernest Board.)
By kind permission of the Bristol Corporation and the Artist

Newfoundland or Cape Breton Island, but no one can be sure. His voyage made a great stir in England at the time, however, as we learn from a letter written by another Italian who was in England then.   He wrote to his brother in Venice :

" Our countryman, the Venetian who went with a ship from Bristol to search for new islands, has returned, and says that, seven hundred leagues from here, he discovered mainland, the territory of the Great Khan.   He coasted it for three hundred leagues and landed ; he saw no human beings, but has brought here to the king certain snares which had been set to catch game, and a needle for making nets ; he also found some chopped trees, by which he judged there were inhabitants. . . . He has been three months on the voyage. . . . On his return he saw two islands to starboard, but would not land, so as not to lose time, for he was short of provisions.   This has greatly pleased the king. . . .

" The king has promised him for the spring ten ships fitted out as he desires, and at his request has conceded him all the prisoners, except those guilty of high treason, to man his fleet. The king has also given him money with which he may amuse himself till that time, and he is now in Bristol with his sons and his wife, who also is a Venetian.   His name is John Cabot, and he is called the Grand Admiral.   Great honour is paid him ; he dresses in silk, and these English run after him like madmen, so that he can enlist as many of them as he pleases, and a number of our own rogues besides.

" The discoverer of these places planted, on the lands he found, a large cross with one flag of England and one of St. Mark, on account of his being a Venetian, so that our banner has stood very far afield."

A second voyage was made, and then Cabot and his sons pass out of the story. We hear nothing further about them, and the Bristol merchants evidently could not find any profitable business in the New Found Land.   It was eighty years before another English expedition set sail for America.

4. A SEAMAN OF ST. MALO

AFTER Columbus and the Cabots had made their voyages to the New World all the monarchs of Europe became anxious to have kingdoms beyond the seas. Most of all they wanted to find a sea route to India and Cathay by sailing westward. Portugal and Spain sent out so many seamen that the monarchs of these two countries decided that they would divide the New World between themselves.

When Francis I., King of France, heard this he laughed heartily and said, " Show me the will of Father Adam by which he left to these two princes the whole of the New World." And straightway he commanded that a French expedition should go to America. A royal commission for discovery and trade was given to a bold seaman of St. Malo, Jacques Cartier, and on May 10, 1534, he and his men sailed away to the westward.

They had a stormy voyage, for not until late July did they bring their ships to anchor in the sheltered harbour of Gaspé. As the Frenchmen erected a cross bearing the arms of France, Indians came stealthily from the forests. Cartier tried to explain to them the meaning of the words " Vive le roi de France." They could not understand him, but they laughed gleefully when he gave them gifts of bright beads, handkerchiefs, and bells.

By means of signs the Indians warned Cartier that soon, very soon, the weather would grow cold and the bay would be blocked with ice. Cartier and his men at once prepared to return to France. As one old chief of the Indians bade Cartier farewell he begged him to return, and Cartier promised, " We will come back next year for a certainty, and will bring you gifts from your new king."

The next year Cartier and his men arrived at Gaspé early in July, and with two Indian guides they proceeded up the " great river of Canada," the St. Lawrence, to the mouth of the Saguenay. Here a throng of Indians in birch-bark canoes were gathered to welcome them, and the Indian chief, Donnacona, escorted Cartier

CARTIER AT STADACONA
(*T. W. Mitchell.*)
By kind permission of Brigdens Ltd., Toronto

to their village of Stadacona, built where to-day stands the city of Quebec.

From Stadacona Cartier and his men, much against the wishes of Donnacona, sailed up the river to another Indian village called Hochelaga, which was built where to-day is the city of Montreal. The Indians of Hochelaga were as glad to see the Frenchmen as the Indians of Stadacona had been, and they invited their visitors to go with them on many hunting expeditions. When Cartier prepared to leave they became as angry and threatening as Donnacona and his braves had been.

Cartier and his men decided to spend the winter in Stadacona, a decision which filled the Indians there with great joy. They took their new " pale-face " friends on many hunting trips, and helped them to build huts for the winter. But at last, in late December, the Frenchmen could no longer hunt, nor could they even chop wood to keep their fires burning. A terrible sickness had broken out among them, and every week for many weeks several men died and others became ill with the dread disease. At first Cartier did not let the Indians know of their trouble, for he feared that they might become frightened and desert them. Finally, however, he met an Indian doctor, who told him to brew tea for his men from the branches of the balsam tree. When they had drunk this tea for six days there was not a sick man among them. " We had brewed a tree as big as a French oak," Cartier wrote in his diary.

In the spring Cartier sailed again for France. When the king heard of the magnificent country of " the Kingdom of Canada," and of the noble river that flowed through it, he said to Cartier, " You must return, and on the banks of the river St. Lawrence establish a colony, a New France beyond the seas."

Although Cartier rejoiced at the commission, and set out bravely with a group of hopeful colonists, the " New France beyond the seas " did not flourish. " They had storehouses, but no stores ; mills, but no grists ; an ample oven, but no bread "—so one historian has described the sad plight of these first settlers in Canada. Disappointed and discouraged, and ill from privation, Cartier took many of the settlers back to France, and there he lived in seclusion for the remaining years of his life.

5. HOW THE INDIANS LIVED

FOR hundreds of years, indeed " for time out of mind," Indians have lived on this continent. We do not know where they came from, nor how many there were when white men first came to America. We do know, however, that there were over fifty large groups or families of them, and that each family spoke a language of its own. In eastern and central Canada there were four of these language groups or families, but west of the Rocky Mountains there were at least eight families of Indians.

The biggest Indian family of Canada was the Algonkian, and to it belonged, among others, the Montagnais tribe, who lived in the eastern foothills of the Rocky Mountains and on the shores of the St. Lawrence. The second largest family was the Iroquoian, and to it belonged both the Hurons and their bitter enemies, the Indians of the Five Nations. These Indians made their homes around Lakes Ontario and Erie, and in the valley of the St. Lawrence. Although the Montagnais Indians were probably the first Indians to see white men, it was the Five Nations and the Hurons who first fought against them and first befriended them.

As a great deal of Canada's early history is connected with the Indians of the Iroquoian family, it is important for us to know something of their manner of living. They were more civilized than the other Indian families, since they lived together and cultivated the soil. They built fortified villages and lived in long wooden huts. They grew crops of corn, maize, and pumpkins. They had many pottery utensils, and their women were very skilful in making beaded ornaments and in basket work. They kept dogs, but had no horses or cattle.

The Five Nations of the Iroquoian family were troublesome and warlike, as indeed were most Indians, with the exception of the Chippewyan tribe of the Lake Athabaska region. Every spring, well armed with bows, arrows, spears, and tomahawks, they set out to fight against their relatives, the Hurons. They fought desperately, and treated their prisoners with great cruelty. When

AN INDIAN VILLAGE.
(*Fergus Kyle.*)

they were ready to make peace they buried a number of tomahawks in sight of their foes to let them know that they were willing to smoke the pipe of peace. When the French came to Canada the Five Nations extended their hatred to them, and they fought against them as bitterly as they did against the Hurons. Usually, after a battle with the Five Nations, the French welcomed an invitation to smoke the pipe of peace.

Indian boys and girls had a care-free life until they were twelve or fourteen years old. Then the boys began their training to be " braves," and the girls were taught cooking, beading, and tanning. Among some of the tribes the girls were taught blanket-weaving. Indian boys and girls played many games which are played by children of to-day, among them cat's-cradle, and battle-dore and shuttlecock. Indians taught the white men at least one game, lacrosse, and many of our pastimes of to-day, such as toboganning, snow-shoeing, and canoeing.

Although the Indians often showed bitter hatred of the white men, the early pioneers of Upper Canada had many reasons for being thankful to them. Many of the trails which led them to their new homes, or which led explorers to the fur-country, were blazed first by Indians. Many pioneers would have starved had it not been that Indians showed them how to preserve the meat of the hunt.

In saying that the Indians of the Iroquoian family were more civilized than most other Indians, we should not forget the Indians of the Pacific coast. The tribes of nearly all their families were skilled in basket work and weaving. Their pottery, too, was very beautiful, both in design and in the colourings which adorned it. One tribe of these Pacific Indians had a code of morals which has been translated into our language, and several of their rules we give here :

It is bad to steal ; people will despise you and say you are poor. . . . They will laugh at you, and will not trust you.

It is bad to boast if you are not great.

It is good to be hospitable, liberal, and friendly.

It is good to be modest and sociable.

6. THE FATHER OF NEW FRANCE

NEARLY sixty years had passed since Cartier had made his last voyage to Canada. Although French and Basque fishermen had come year by year to the Newfoundland fishing-banks, the kings of France seemed to have quite forgotten their possessions in North America. A long and bitter civil war had made it difficult to send any further expeditions.

At last France had a strong and skilful king, Henry IV., who was able to take up once more the work of exploring and settling the land discovered by Cartier.

Samuel Champlain had already made several voyages to America before he led an expedition to found a settlement at Quebec. At the foot of the cliff he built a roomy " habitation," as he called it, with separate store-rooms, a stockade around his buildings, and a wharf. A garden was planted, and a trade in furs done with the Indians. But Champlain was not a mere trader ; exploration was his main interest.

He made friends with the Hurons and Algonquins who lived near by, and with them journeyed up the St. Lawrence. Then turning south they paddled and portaged up the Richelieu River. This brought them to a large and beautiful lake surrounded by high wooded hills. To this lake Champlain, as its discoverer, gave his own name.

Now the Hurons and Algonquins were at deadly enmity with the Iroquois, who lived in the country south of Lake Ontario and the Upper St. Lawrence. Lake Champlain was in their territory, and it was not long before Champlain and his friends came to blows with one of their war-parties.

Thanks to the firearms of the white men, which were used for the first time and with deadly effect on the Iroquois, the Hurons were victorious and made quite a hero of Champlain. Although their friendship was indispensable to Champlain's struggling colony, it was unfortunate that another consequence of the fight was the

[PLATE 6.

CHAMPLAIN AT GEORGIAN BAY
(Charles W. Jefferys.)

bitter enmity of the Iroquois, which brought terror and bloodshed to New France for over a hundred years.

The difficulties of the new colony kept Champlain so busy that it was four years before he could go exploring again. This time he went up the Ottawa River, because another Frenchman had told him a story of having found the sea at a distance of only fourteen days' journey. Although the story turned out to be a pure invention, it led to Champlain making the most important geographical discovery of his career. Pushing up the Ottawa River, the Indian guides led him, by an intricate route of lake and stream and portage, to the open waters of Lake Nipissing. Out of that lake flows the French River into Lake Huron, and Champlain was the first white man to behold the myriads of islands which are scattered over Georgian Bay. Thus he took the first great step in unfolding the vast panorama of the West.

When Champlain was preparing to return to Quebec his Huron friends came into conflict with their deadly enemies, the Iroquois, and in the battle Champlain was wounded. He had to spend the winter in a Huron encampment, and when, in the late spring, he returned to Quebec, he found that he had been mourned as dead.

During his absence new settlers had come to Quebec, among them the Hébert family who settled on a little farm close to the fort, and were the first to make their living from the soil. New houses were built and fortifications strengthened and extended. In the year 1629, when the little colony was beginning to feel safe from the famine that had threatened it, a new danger arose. An English fleet sailed into the harbour and claimed Quebec for England. Champlain bravely refused to surrender, but in a few days he was forced to give way and to become a prisoner of the English admiral, David Kirke.

Three years later, after Quebec was restored to France, he returned to the colony, and for the two remaining years of his life he devoted all his time to building up the little settlements he had founded. When he died, on Christmas day in the year 1635, he had well earned the title by which he is known to-day, that of Father of New France.

7. HENRY HUDSON

AMONG the many brave men who sailed the seas in search of a North-West Passage to China and India, none has written his name so prominently on the map as Henry Hudson. His life was a hard one, his reward was meagre, and his end was tragic. But no explorer has a more enduring monument than the great inland sea, Hudson Bay, that forms the northern approach to Canada, or the mighty river that also bears his name.

We know nothing of his early life. His first appearance in history is while commanding an expedition to discover a North-East Passage to Asia. That purpose failed, but Nova Zemlya and Spitsbergen were explored. Then, in the year 1609, he crossed the Atlantic and discovered the Hudson River. This was in the same year that Champlain first navigated his lake, so the two explorers, without knowing it, were perhaps within two hundred miles of each other. Had they met, it would have been an interesting occasion.

Next year he set out again, this time to seek a passage westward round the northern coast of America.

Rounding the southern point of Greenland, he sailed west, and found the entrance to Hudson Strait. Beset by huge icebergs, baffled by fog and by treacherous currents, he managed to bring his little ship safely through the Strait to the calmer waters of the Bay. His crew was frightened and unruly. The compass was behaving strangely owing to the nearness of the Magnetic Pole, but of course they did not understand the reason, and their confidence in the captain was destroyed. The rest of the summer was spent in patiently exploring the eastern coast of the Bay, and autumn found him at the southern extremity of James Bay. Ice was already forming, and it was too late to reach the open sea. So Hudson made his ship as safe as possible, and prepared for the Arctic winter.

They were ill-provided to withstand the cold, and were ignorant

HUDSON CAST ADRIFT
(*J. R. Skelton.*)

of how to make the best of what they had.   The temper of the men got worse, and soon they realized they were threatened with death by starvation.   A skilful hunter might have saved them, and things looked more hopeful when an Indian appeared on the scene. They traded some knives for fresh meat, but the Indian never returned with the additional supplies which he had promised.

By springtime, which is June in those latitudes, their food was reduced to starvation rations.   They set sail for England, doubting whether they could get there before they starved to death.

Then a cruel and dastardly plot was formed by some of the mutinous sailors.   Since there was not food enough for all, they determined to get rid of as many as they could before proceeding farther on their voyage.

Early one morning, as the captain came out on deck, he was seized and bound by some of the crew.   A boat was lowered, and after a sharp struggle in which four men were killed, all who were sick or were loyal to the captain were forced to leave the ship—even Hudson's young son was not spared.   The boat was cast adrift.   Without food, drink, fire, or sufficient clothing, in an open boat on an ice-covered sea, their fate would be sure and swift.

Hudson faced his murderers with a manly courage.   Even more admirable was the splendid loyalty of Philip Staffe, the ship's carpenter.   Although he might have remained unharmed on board the ship, he chose to follow his captain to certain death rather than desert him.

We are not sorry to learn that the mutineers, without their leader, had a dreadful return voyage.   Through their ignorance they nearly lost the ship, and only nine starving survivors reached the shores of England.

8. THE PILGRIM FATHERS

EARLY in the seventeenth century King James I. of England commanded all his subjects to become members of the Church of England. At this time in England there were many people, called Puritans, who did not wish to worship God in the manner of the Church of England. Instead of going to church these people met in chapels or out in the open fields, to hold services of their own. Here they sang hymns that their leaders had made for them, and prayed in their own simple words. When the king heard this, and was told that they refused to obey his command, he sent soldiers to break up their meetings and to arrest their leaders and preachers.

Now in Holland people were permitted to worship God as they chose, and many of the Dutch people were Puritans, so the English Puritans decided to go there to live. The Dutch people welcomed them very kindly to their city of Leyden, and helped them to find work. But the English men and women were not altogether happy in Holland. They longed for a country of their own, and for this reason they decided to go on a bold venture. They would go to America—to that rich and beautiful land, Virginia.

.　　　　.　　　　.　　　　.　　　　.　　　　.

On September 5, 1620, a little ship, bearing the name of *Mayflower*, was lying at anchor in Plymouth harbour. During the day men, women, and children went on board carrying heavy travelling bags and parcels. These people were Puritans who had returned to England from Holland, and on the morrow they were to sail for America. That night at dusk these " Pilgrims," for that was the name given to them, bade farewell to their friends, and before dawn the next morning the frail little boat put out to sea.

The tiny ship was buffeted by many storms. All through September and October the sailors toiled at the ropes and the sails.

THE PILGRIM FATHERS.
(*George Morrow.*)

With November came heavy gales, and the ship was driven far northward. Instead of landing in Virginia, the weary Pilgrims disembarked on the shores of what is now called New England. It was a bleak, barren shore, and not far away were gloomy forests.

Many of the Pilgrims were sick, and all of them were sadly disheartened. But they could not turn back; already ice was forming along the shores, and they could only set to work building rough cabins and chopping wood for winter fires. They were afraid of the Indians who peered out at them from the forest, and of the strange wild animals that lurked in its depths.

They spent a terrible winter. Never before had they suffered such cold, and never before had they known such pitiful sickness and loneliness.

At last spring came. The ice melted. The trees became green and beautiful. Birds sang, and merry little forest animals began to run about. With the coming of spring new hope filled the Pilgrims. They cut down trees, ploughed the land, and sowed corn. When their seed was sown they made a palisade about their village, and during the summer they built a little chapel.

In the autumn, when their crops were harvested, they gathered together in their chapel for a day of Thanksgiving. It was a day of great rejoicing, for they had many things which made them thankful. Their crops were good; they had made friends with the Indians; sickness had almost disappeared from their homes; they had founded a " New England " in America. But more than for anything else they thanked God that they could now worship Him in their own way. This was the first Thanksgiving Day, and ever since then people have been setting aside one day of the year at harvest time, to give thanks to God for goodly crops and comfortable, happy homes.

9. THE MISSIONS OF THE JESUITS

IN the spring of 1625 a ship arrived before the great cliffs of Quebec. Among the passengers were the first Jesuit missionaries to come to Canada. They were Fathers Lalement, Massé, and Brébœuf, and two lay brothers of the Society.

For a few months the five missionaries worked together in Quebec. They had several Indian interpreters to teach them the language of the Hurons and Algonquins, and with these Indians as their guides they made expeditions into the neighbouring country. Before winter set in Father Brébœuf joined a party of hunters and went with them to their winter village. He lived with these Indians until spring, learning their language and customs, and telling them of God and Christ.

In the spring, when the village was broken up, he joined a party of Hurons going west and north to the district about Lake Simcoe and Georgian Bay. For three years Father Brébœuf never left his mission field. He taught the Indian children, nursed the sick, and worked diligently translating the catechism into the language of the Hurons.

It was a hard, lonely life he lived. The Indians gave little heed to his teaching, and at times they became very angry with him. When the Iroquois attacked them they said that " the white devil " was to blame, and when their crops failed they said that the cross on the chapel had cast a spell over their land.

Despite discouragement and loneliness, Father Brébœuf never gave up his purpose, and at last a few Indians came to love him for his kindness and gentle teaching. When he was joined by Father Daniel, a young priest who had lately arrived from France, the Indians gave him a friendly welcome. For nearly four years he ministered in a village not far from the shores of Lake Simcoe, but on one fateful morning, when he had his flock gathered in the chapel, a wild cry rang out, " The Iroquois ! The Iroquois ! " and almost in the twinkling of an eye the bloodthirsty enemies of

A JESUIT MISSIONARY.
(E. J. Dinsmore.)

the Hurons broke into the chapel and set it on fire. There was no way of escape, and Father Daniel and his parishioners perished in the flames.

But this tragedy did not drive Father Brébœuf from his mission field. A new assistant was sent to him from Quebec, Father Lalement, a nephew of that Father Lalement who came to Canada with Brébœuf, and they worked together for nearly ten years. They built twelve mission stations and seven chapels, and had several hundreds of true converts.

But, just when they were gaining confidence and hope, the old enemies of the Hurons again went on the war-path. With dreadful screams and war-whoops the Iroquois attacked the frontier village of the Hurons. They came in the dead of night, and in the morning there was nothing left of the village but smouldering ashes. Fathers Brébœuf and Lalement were taken prisoners and brutally murdered.

After their death the mission to Huronia was abandoned, but the Jesuits did not give up their purpose. Father Jogues stayed at his post at Sault Ste. Marie, ministering to the Algonquins until the Iroquois took him prisoner. After he was released he went to the Iroquois on a mission of peace, and for a time he was able to live among them and teach them.

There were many other brave priests who journeyed into the unknown country to minister to the Indians. Among them was Father Marquette, who along with a young Canadian trader, Louis Jolliet, went westward and south into the land of the Mississippi.

The Jesuit missionaries spread the Gospel from Hudson Bay to the Gulf of Mexico, and from the Atlantic to the Pacific. Their story truly is " one of the most glorious and tragic pages of Canadian history."

10. THE FOUNDING OF MONTREAL

On a hot August day in the year 1641 a little vessel came slowly into the harbour of Quebec. Governor de Montmagny, who had succeeded Champlain as governor of New France, went himself to the quay to welcome the unexpected guests. The leader of the group of travellers at once explained their reason for coming to New France.

"Your scheme is impossible," Monsieur Montmagny said, when Sieur de Maisonneuve had finished speaking. "Mont Royale is too far from Quebec, and too near the Iroquois country for you to build a city."

"Nevertheless we shall go," Maisonneuve replied, "even if every tree were an Iroquois."

And so in the spring of the next year, despite the warnings of Governor Montmagny, Maisonneuve and his company of forty set off boldly up the St. Lawrence. In the early morning of the 17th of May they landed on the island where, over a hundred years before, Cartier had discovered the Indian village of Hochelaga. But now there was no sign of the village or of any human abode. The air was still, and the grass was richly green, decked with bright May flowers. Indeed the whole scene was such as to give comfort and peace to the new-comers, who now fell upon their knees and thanked Almighty God for His goodness in bringing them safely to the island of Mont Royale.

Among Maisonneuve's faithful company there were at least two others who were filled with a pious zeal equal to that of their leader. They were Father Vimont, a Jesuit priest, and Mademoiselle Jeanne Mance. These people had come to Mont Royale to build a city, not that they or their friends in France might become wealthy by trade with the Indians, but that they might live among the Indians and teach them the lessons of Christianity. So after the stockade was erected it was not a fort that was next built but a hospital, and in it, for nearly all the remaining years of

THE FOUNDING OF MONTREAL
(Fergus Kyle.)

her long life, Mademoiselle Mance ministered to sick and suffering Indians.

For two years the little settlement of Ville Marie was left in peace and quiet. Then on a fateful spring morning the Iroquois drew close to the walls of the city. When Maisonneuve was warned of their approach, he marshalled his forces and marched out boldly to meet them. No sooner were the Frenchmen beyond the gates than they were assailed by flying arrows and bullets. Tomahawks gleamed from unseen hands and war-cries rent the air. The amazed Frenchmen, who had no experience of this kind of warfare, retreated to the walls of the city.

The last man to reach the gates was Maisonneuve, and as he was about to enter, he was attacked by a chief of the Iroquois. For a moment the two brave, dauntless men stared at each other, and then, as the Indian brandished his tomahawk in the air, Maisonneuve raised his pistol. Before the oncoming Iroquois realized what had happened their chief had fallen and the gates of the town were closed.

To-day, in the city of Montreal, you may see the very place of the encounter. It is called the Place d'Armes, and there is a statue of the brave Maisonneuve who first saved Ville Marie from the Iroquois.

Despite suffering and loneliness, the zealous founders of the city persevered until, when Jeanne Mance died, the city had become a thriving outpost of French civilization, its brave workers esteemed by the French and reverenced by the Indians.

11. THE HEROES OF THE LONG SAULT

THE Iroquois hated the French very bitterly, and after they had destroyed many villages of Huronia and killed the missionaries, they decided to attack the little settlement at Montreal. Word of their wicked plot was brought to Montreal by a group of fleeing Algonquins, and when the governor heard it he was sadly distressed and greatly perplexed. What could he do ? Montreal had but a feeble garrison.

It was then that Adam Daulac, a brave young Frenchman who had been a *coureur de bois*, sought out the governor and said, " I, with sixteen of my true friends, will go out to meet the enemy."

At first Maisonneuve would not listen to his petition. He shook his head and said, " No, no, my friend. I cannot grant you permission to go forth to certain death, and to take with you sixteen brave men. New France has need of living men. There is nought that we can do but watch and pray."

Daulac and his friends were firm in their purpose, and at last the governor gave his consent. They, with all the people of Ville Marie for witnesses, swore a solemn oath to give or take no quarter, but to fight to their last breath to save their beloved settlement. Then they paddled up to the Ottawa River until they came to the Long Sault Rapids, near which they found a deserted fort, well hidden in the dense forest, and there they decided to wait for the enemy. Nor did they have long to wait, for in a few days they saw the Iroquois canoes coming toward them. They came so swiftly that the Frenchmen, who were cooking their dinner in the open, did not have time to carry their pots and kettles back into the fort.

With much shouting, for they were certain of an easy victory over so small a band of white men, the Indians came ashore at once, and approached the crumbling walls of the fort. But no sooner were they within range than the French rained bullets on them. They could do naught but hurry away in confusion, and for three days and three nights they waited in ambush to see some

DEFENCE OF THE LONG SAULT
(*Henry Sandham.*)

weakening within the fort. Several times they ventured forth, but each time they were driven back by a steady hail of French bullets.

Within the fort every one was calm and quiet, but there was great suffering, for the brave men had no food other than dry cornmeal, and they had no water. Each day they grew weaker, and at last, when the Indians advanced, carrying branches of trees to screen them from sight, the French heroes saw that they were vanquished ; but they did not yield. They died fighting for their friends and for the little settlement of Ville Marie.

These seventeen young men have ever since been called the " Heroes of the Long Sault," for although they were not victorious in their struggle, they did succeed in saving the little colony at Montreal.

" If seventeen white men behind a battered wooden fence can hold seven hundred warriors at bay, what will a hundred white men behind a stone wall do to us ? " the Indians asked. And so, frightened and disheartened, they returned to their homes, and for a time left Montreal in peace.

12. THE GREAT INTENDANT

" Cause justice to reign, protect the inhabitants, discipline them
against enemies, and procure for them peace, repose, and plenty."
—Jean Baptiste Talon thought of these words many times on
his voyage to New France, for they were the instructions given
to him when his king, Louis XIV., made him intendant, or
superintendent, of New France.

Jean Talon came to New France about thirty years after Champlain's death, and he came determined to be " as true to the people
of New France as that gallant pioneer had been." From his first
days in the country he spent little time in his comfortable home in
Quebec. In a birch-bark canoe, and with an Indian guide, he
travelled throughout the colony. He talked to farmers about their
crops and about the land they were breaking. They showed him
their cattle and their barns, and he even went into madame's
kitchen to learn how she dried corn and vegetables, and preserved
wild fruits.

The message, " M. Talon has come," was welcome news in
any little settlement, for the people knew he would listen to their
troubles and give them wise, fatherly advice. They knew, too,
that he would tell them of their dear homeland, and that he would
have words of encouragement and comfort for them from the king
himself. " The king has commanded me to tell you," Talon
would say to them, " that he loves you as his own children. He
rejoices in your prosperity and sorrows with you in your pain and
grief."

On his first visit among the settlers M. Talon saw that cattle,
horses, and sheep were needed. He asked the king to send out
shiploads of them, and when they came he summoned the settlers
to a great market in Quebec. They came on foot, in canoes, and
in ox-carts, and to each one he gave, in the name of the king,
whatever animals he needed most.

Not long after the horses, cows, and sheep were distributed

A VISIT OF THE INTENDANT.
(*L. R. Batchelor.*)
By kind permission of the Dominion Archives, Ottawa.

Talon sent to France for hemp seed. The farmers planted it and used the hemp to make coarse cloth. He encouraged the women on the farms to learn to spin and weave wool and the men to tan leather. In one letter which he sent to the king he said, " I am now clothed from head to foot in apparel all made in New France."

Although M. Talon knew that farming should be the chief work of the settlers, he wanted the farmers' sons to learn a trade. He decided to build a ship, therefore, and in the autumn of 1666 he asked the young men to come to Quebec to help with the building. When the ship was fitted out for sea, M. Talon sent it laden with staves, planks, cod, salmon, and fish oil, to trade with the West Indies. A cargo of sugar was brought back in return.

One thing which Talon planned and undertook shows very well that he had great confidence in our country. He set men to work to build a highway from Quebec to Acadia. The road was not completed in Talon's lifetime, nor, indeed, for many decades afterward, but nevertheless it is interesting to know that the " Great Intendant " was the first to begin building Canadian highways.

Jean Baptiste Talon did many other things to help the people of New France to be happy and prosperous in their new homes, and from this brief account you will know that he might well be called " The Father of Canadian Industry and Trade."

13. "THE COMPANY OF ADVENTURERS TRADING INTO HUDSON'S BAY"

On a day in June in the year 1670, nearly sixty years after Henry Hudson had sailed away from the same harbour, an expedition left Gravesend for Hudson Bay, led by two dauntless Frenchmen. Their names were Pierre Radisson and Henri Groseilliers, and they were as resolute in their purpose and as confident of success as Hudson had been. King Charles of England had given them a royal charter, and seventeen of his wealthiest subjects had become directors of their Company. These men, with the noble Prince Rupert at their head, were called "The Governor and Company of Adventurers of England Trading into Hudson's Bay," and not only they, but many people in England, expected these two Frenchmen to bring thousands of furs to England every year.

"Six hundred thousand beaver skins! Remember! Six hundred thousand beaver skins next year!" the people on the shore shouted in farewell, and the men on the ship laughed jubilantly and promised even more than six hundred thousand.

And no wonder they were so happy and confident, for King Charles had given them the sole right to trade in the vast area which extends from Hudson Bay to Alaska, and from Alaska to California. They were to hunt, trap, build forts, make friends with the Indians, and at all times to explore the country and to search diligently for the North-West Passage to the Orient.

That year Radisson and Groseilliers and their English workers journeyed far into the great country west of Hudson Bay. They built three forts, and sent out many runners to tell the Indians about the guns, blankets, sugar, and bright trinkets they had in their stores. In the spring, when they sent their cargoes of furs to England, King Charles and Prince Rupert and the seventeen directors of the Company were so pleased that they commanded them to build more forts, and to go even farther into the vast country. Many years afterward it was said that there was not a

INDIANS VISITING FORT CHARLES, 1670
By kind permission of the Hudson's Bay Company

lake or a stream that did not have a Hudson's Bay Company fort or trading-post on its shores. In the spring, as soon as the ice broke, the Indians came in their canoes, laden with heavy pelts, to trade at these forts. Then shortly afterward several sturdy ships would set sail from Hudson Bay for England.

At first the beaver-skin was considered the most valuable, and a table of exchange values was made out for the trader. With one beaver-skin an Indian might buy a half-pound of brightly coloured beads, or one pound of tobacco or five pounds of sugar. For four beaver-skins he might have a gallon of brandy, twelve large buttons or twenty fish-hooks. For twelve beaver-skins he might have a gun.

Such were the beginnings of the great " Company of Adventurers of England Trading into Hudson's Bay." For many decades this company, which later came to be called the Hudson's Bay Company, ruled over the vast territory extending from Hudson Bay to the Arctic Ocean and to the shores of the Pacific. Many brave explorers went out from the Company's forts to search for the North-West Passage, and incidentally to look for rare metals. One of the most courageous explorers of the Company was James Knight, whose sad fate was not known until fifty years later. Another explorer of the Company was Henry Kelsey, about whom we shall read in the next section.

14. A COMMISSION OF DISCOVERY

IT is the year 1683. A tiny ship is leaving the Port of London, and on its deck two persons, a man and a boy, stand watching the shores disappear in the haze. The man is Pierre Radisson, one of the founders of the Hudson's Bay Company, and the boy is a London street urchin, Henry Kelsey.

After the shores of England vanish, and their course is laid to the westward, the timid boy asks the famous explorer many questions. Will he be allowed to have a canoe ? Are the Indians really dangerous ? Will he be permitted to explore the strange new land, or will he have to stay at Fort Nelson ?

Radisson cannot answer all his questions, but instead he tells him many tales of his own adventures, tales so thrilling that the boy's eyes sparkle with excitement, and he exclaims eagerly, " I am going to be an explorer like you, sir, and I, too, shall be a friend of the Indians."

But alas for poor Henry Kelsey's dreams of adventures and Indian friendships ! For four years he lived a weary life at Fort Nelson. He was seldom allowed to go beyond the gates of the fort, and twice, when he did climb over the barricades and dash after some Indians, he was brought back by a party of searchers.

Then one day, when the yearly mail came from England, a wonderful thing happened to young Henry Kelsey. Captain Geyer, the chief trader of the fort, sent for him and read these words to him : " The boy Henry Kelsey is to be sent to the Churchill River with Thomas Savage because we are informed that he is a very active lad, delighting much in Indian company, being never better pleased than when he is travelling amongst them."

It couldn't be true ! He must be dreaming ! But no, there were the words—he could read them for himself. At last, after four years of restlessness and impatience, he was to become an explorer.

KELSEY SIGHTS THE BUFFALO
(*Charles W. Jefferys.*)
By kind permission of the Hudson's Bay Company

In July 1689 Henry Kelsey and the young Cree brave, Thomas Savage, set out from Fort Nelson on their expedition of discovery. They went to the mouth of the Churchill River, and from there they travelled far inland without seeing any one or finding any animal other than the musk-ox. The next year young Kelsey was sent into the country of the Assiniboines, with instructions " to call, encourage, and invite the remoter Indians to trade with us." These were Captain Geyer's commands, and two years later he had every reason to be pleased with the manner in which they had been carried out, for Kelsey returned to the fort with a " good fleet of Indians," and a valuable cargo of beaver pelts.

Kelsey had no surveying instruments, and so it was impossible for Captain Geyer to have more than a general idea of where he had been. Kelsey kept a diary, however, and from it we know now that he went to the lower reaches of the Saskatchewan River and journeyed over what is now the eastern part of the Province of Saskatchewan.

By his journey north he had been the first Englishman to see the musk-ox; so on the prairie he was the first Englishman to see the vast herds of buffalo.

Kelsey's diary was lost for over a hundred years. Recently it was found in a castle in Northern Ireland. In it we may read the first account ever written of the buffalo hunt. Kelsey was, moreover, the first white man to visit the western tribes, and the first to attempt any exploration of the great plains stretching west to the Rockies for thousands of miles.

15. " MY GUNS WILL GIVE MY ANSWER "

FLAGS were flying in Quebec; happy people in gaily-coloured dresses and uniforms were hurrying towards the harbour. As a little ship came up the river they clapped their hands and shouted, " See! There he is! See! Our governor has returned to us." So on a July day in the year 1689 Count Frontenac was welcomed back to New France. He had been away for nearly ten years—a sad, troublous ten years it had been for the people of the little colony—but now, as he walked among them, they felt their old confidence returning.

But alas! their troubles were not over. Scarcely had the people finished telling him of the terrible raid that the Iroquois had made only a few weeks before on the village of La Chine, than another danger threatened the little colony. Before Frontenac had time to receive his friends at the governor's mansion, an English sea captain, Sir William Phips, anchored his fleet of thirty-four ships below Quebec, and demanded the instant surrender of the city.

" My general expects a reply by eleven," the English officer, who had been sent ashore, said to Count Frontenac.

" He need not wait so long," Frontenac replied haughtily. " I refuse to surrender."

" Will you put it in writing ? " the officer asked.

" Writing ! " Frontenac exclaimed scornfully. " My guns will give my answer."

Frontenac's bold words made the officer think that Quebec was well protected by soldiers and arms, and within two days the English sailed away to Boston. Once more Frontenac had saved the little colony from her enemies.

No wonder, then, that the people trusted him and loved him dearly. No wonder that, when he had been recalled to France, they sent constant messages to the king begging him to let Frontenac

" MY GUNS WILL GIVE MY ANSWER "—FRONTENAC, 1690.
(*Henry Sandham.*)

return to them.   " He can save us when no one else can," they said to the king, " for the Indians fear him and respect him, and we ourselves have a great faith in him."

Elsewhere you may read of the many bold undertakings of the gallant Count Frontenac, who was first made governor of New France in the year 1672.

Perhaps the most interesting thing you will learn of him, is how he won the friendship of the Iroquois who, for over fifty years, had been the bitter enemies of the French.   He did this, not by making war on them, but by summoning them to a great meeting at Cataraqui, and there talking to them in friendly fashion. While he talked to them and went among them, giving the women and children gifts, the men who had come to Cataraqui with him felled trees, squared timbers, and built a strong fort, where, to-day, is the city of Kingston.   To this fort he invited the Iroquois to bring their furs, and from this fort the fur-traders were able to get stores of supplies for their long journeys.

Although Frontenac was fiery tempered and wilful, he was just and kind ; you will learn, too, that, although he loved splendour and wanted every one to stand in awe of him, he had the foresight and the perseverance of a great empire-builder.

16. THE DARING LA SALLE

WHEN Frontenac became governor of New France he was anxious to build up an empire extending far west from Montreal and far south from Quebec. There were many French adventurers who wanted to go on voyages of discovery, but Frontenac had more confidence in one of them than in all the others. This man was a keen-eyed youth from Rouen, named René Robert Cavelier, Sieur de La Salle.

From the time he was a little boy La Salle had heard of New France, for his brother was a priest in Montreal, and he had read of many daring expeditions sent out to search for the western passage to China. No wonder, then, that René did not choose to be either a priest, as his brother was, or a merchant, like his father. He decided to be an explorer, and his quest was the North-West Passage to the Orient.

When La Salle came to New France men were talking of the " great water " which the Indians called the Mississippi. When he heard of it La Salle and his friend Tonti decided to explore this river, " for," said La Salle, " so mighty a river must surely lead to the Western Ocean, and thence at last we shall reach the China Seas."

Before La Salle began his explorations he built a ship on the shores of Lake Erie. This ship he called the *Griffon*, in honour of Count Frontenac, whose coat-of-arms was adorned by figures of these mythical animals. In the early spring of the year 1680 the *Griffon* sailed out into the waters of Lake Erie, and thence into Lake Michigan, the first sailing craft to pass over the waters of the Great Lakes. She was then laden with furs and sent back to Lake Erie, to return with supplies for his further travels.

But alas! the good ship, strong though she was and captained by one of the bravest sailors of France, was wrecked in the stormy waters of Lake Michigan, and La Salle and Tonti were left to make their way onward as best they could. When they were

THE BUILDING OF THE " GRIFFON "
(*Fergus Kyle.*)

faced with hunger and mutiny, La Salle turned back to Montreal for supplies, and it was not until the next year that they were ready to embark on the Mississippi.

The weather was cold and stormy when they left the shores of Lake Michigan, but each day as they floated down-stream the air grew warmer, birds sang, flowers bloomed, and on the day they reached the mouth of the great river the air was heavy with heat and the ground was covered with luxurious verdure.

But again La Salle was disappointed, for the great river had brought him not to the Western Ocean but to the Gulf of Mexico. On its shores La Salle and Tonti raised a pillar, and upon it they carved the arms of France and the words, " Louis the Great, King of France and Navarre, April 9, 1682."

La Salle had failed in his purpose, but he had taken a vast country for France. When King Louis heard of the new land, which La Salle had called Louisiana, he was so pleased that he gave him ships and money to go on another expedition in search of the passage to China. This expedition failed dismally ; two of the ships were lost, and food was stolen ; the men of the crew mutinied, and on the shores of the Gulf of Mexico the angry and starving men slew their brave leader. So ended the career of René Robert La Salle ; his brilliant dream never came true, but he founded a kingdom for France, and helped to make her great among the nations of the world.

17. MADELEINE DE VERCHÈRES

THE Seigneury of Verchères was ten miles from Montreal. Its broad acres, sloping gently to the St. Lawrence, were among the first to be cultivated after Maisonneuve had founded the city. The Seigneur of Verchères lived on his estate, but every autumn he went to serve in the army.

In the year 1691, just two years after Count Frontenac had returned to New France, the Seigneur of Verchères left his farm early in October. This year Madame de Verchères accompanied him as far as Montreal, where she was to spend at least two weeks in shopping and visiting her friends.

On the morning that the Seigneur and his wife were leaving on their journey, the family was astir long before daybreak. Madeleine helped her mother to pack her travelling bag, and her two little brothers helped to carry parcels to the boat. When everything was in readiness the family went together to the quay, and as the boat was about to pull away Madame said to Madeleine, " Now, my child, you are mistress of the Seigneury. You must look after your brothers and you must be brave."

The first days after their parents were gone were happy days for the Verchères children. They helped to husk corn and pile wood in the yard. Madeleine made several visits to the cottages of the habitants, and, like an experienced mistress, she talked to the women of their work and their children.

Then one day, as Madeleine went into the fields, a man called out, " Run, miss, run! The Iroquois! They come! "

She turned to look, and there, quite close to her, were more dark faces than she cared to count—fifty, perhaps a hundred, and all of them cruel and wicked. Madeleine ran very fast to the fort.

There were two soldiers within the fort, but when Madeleine arrived they could not be seen. At last she found them hiding in terror in a dark corner of the block-house, and saw that they were about to set fire to their store of gunpowder.

"THE FORT HAS BEEN IN GOOD HANDS."
(*Allan Stewart.*)

" Miserable cowards," she exclaimed, " leave this place at once ! " Thoroughly ashamed of themselves, they went to the fort, and as they went the gallant call of Madeleine to her brothers rang in their ears : " Remember what father told us. In the face of danger, fight for God and the king."

Madeleine, her brothers, and the two soldiers began to fire on the Indians. They fired so well that the Indians decided to leave the fort and to turn their attention to the people in the fields.

" Go quickly," Madeleine said to one of the soldiers, " and fire a cannon from the palisade, so that our people may be warned." Soon the people came rushing to the fort, and for each one of them Madeleine had words of comfort. She had need of all her courage, for that night a blinding hailstorm arose, and all within the fort were certain that the Indians would try to climb over the palisades.

All night long her brothers, from their positions on the bastions, kept up a regular call of " All's well ! All's well ! " The Indians, prowling about in the near-by forest, heard the cry and were afraid to attack the palisades.

The siege lasted for over a week. The people became ill with fear and hunger. At last, one night, Madeleine's young brother called to her softly, " Madeleine, listen. I hear something." She listened. She could hear the soft lapping of oars. She peered into the darkness, and could see—could it be ? Yes, it was a little boat drawing to the quay. She and her brothers watched men disembark, and then Madeleine shouted, " Who are you ? "

The answer came back, " We are Frenchmen, come to bring you help."

Madeleine opened the gates at once and rushed to the river. " I surrender the fort to you, sir," she said to the captain.

" It has been in good hands," the soldier made reply.

" But we are glad to give you command," Madeleine said with a smile, " for we have held it for a week."

18. A CLUE TO THE WESTERN SEA

AT the lonely trading-post on Lake Nipigon, under Pierre Gualtier de Varennes, Sieur de la Vérendrye, the old Indian chief Ochagach was always a welcome visitor. As he spread out his furs, he told tales of great warriors and of strange distant lands.

" I will tell you of a lake that is in the land of the setting sun," he said one day, pointing westward. " It is a big lake, and from it a river runs far west, until it comes to another lake, and on this other lake large ships sail, and its waters are filled with salt."

From the time he was a child at Three Rivers, La Vérendrye had heard tales of the Western Sea. French explorers had been seeking it since the days of Cartier, and as he listened to Ochagach he thought that, at last, he had the clue. He would find the Western Sea !

So in the early summer of the year 1731 La Vérendrye, with his three sons and his nephew, set out on their voyage to the Western Sea. They were very happy and confident as their flotilla of birch-bark canoes went up the Ottawa River, for the governor of Quebec had given them a monopoly of the fur trade in the new country, and several rich men in Montreal had provided them with money and goods for trade.

Before the end of their second year in the new country they had built three forts between Lakes Superior and Winnipeg, and they had sent rich cargoes of furs to Montreal.

The Montreal merchants were so pleased that they urged La Vérendrye to continue westward. In a few years more he had built Fort Rouge, where Winnipeg now stands, and a fort on the Assiniboine River, where now is the city of Portage la Prairie.

When he went to Montreal to report to the merchants he said, " I have built a line of forts right into the heart of the fur country. The country between Kaministikwia and Lake Winnipeg has every kind of fur-bearing animal. I tell you the herds of buffalo darken the green earth as far as the eye can see."

Though the merchants would have been satisfied with the

A CLUE TO THE WESTERN SEA
(E. J. Dinsmore.)

furs from this vast country, La Vérendrye was not content. He and his sons were anxious to push on to the Western Sea. They became so much interested in exploration that they forgot how angry the merchants in Montreal would be if they did not continue to receive rich cargoes of furs.

At last, after La Vérendrye had made several journeys westward, the merchants of Montreal and the governor of Quebec summoned him to appear before them. " You can no longer have the monopoly of furs," the governor told him, and the merchants as angrily said, " We will give you no more money or goods."

By this time La Vérendrye was an old man, but he was still brave and confident that the Western Sea was " just beyond, just over the Shining Mountains " which his sons had discovered the year before.

For two years he stayed in Quebec, trying to persuade other merchants to give him supplies. Finally a group of wealthy men gave him money, and he began to prepare for another western voyage. But alas, just as his stores were being packed into his canoes, the gallant explorer was seized by a severe illness and died.

This is the story of a man of great courage and firm purpose. He did not find the Western Sea, but he and his sons did discover and open up a large part of North America.

19. THE FOUNDING OF HALIFAX

WHEN the Cabots reached the shores of North America in the year 1498, they claimed the land for King Henry VII. of England. For over a hundred years, however, no Englishman came to its shores, and the King of England might easily have forgotten about it had he not been reminded of it by one of his Scottish advisers, Sir William Alexander.

" Your Majesty already has a New England beyond the seas," he said to King James, " and now I beg of you to found a New Scotland."

King James liked the idea very much, so he at once gave Sir William Alexander a grant of the land of the Acadian Peninsula.

" It is yours for trade and exploration," he promised. " It is to be called not New Scotland but Nova Scotia, in honour of the language which I love dearly."

So for several years a ship was sent once a year to Nova Scotia from England, but little effort was made to build up a settlement or to explore the country. Indeed, in 1632, when King Charles gave Nova Scotia to France, there was only one man who was angry and regretful. He was Charles La Tour, a French nobleman who had given up his French allegiance and become an English baronet of the Order of Nova Scotia.

For nearly a hundred years France owned Nova Scotia, and when the English regained possession of it they had a better knowledge of its value as a gateway to the vast land beyond. They realized, too, that they must take steps to defend it, for the French, from their fort at Louisburg, were able at any time to make an attack on the almost unprotected English colony in Nova Scotia.

In 1748, therefore, King George II. of England issued a proclamation announcing that a free passage and land would be given to all retired men of the army and navy who would settle in Nova Scotia. He promised them protection from enemies and supplies of ammunition and stores of food for one year. In a

THE FOUNDING OF HALIFAX
(*Charles W. Jefferys.*)

very short time over 2,500 settlers with their families were ready to leave for Nova Scotia.

These settlers were led by an English soldier, Lord Cornwallis, who was renowned for his strength of purpose and his loving care of all the people entrusted to him. They landed in the harbour of Chebuctoo in the summer of 1749, and at once they began to build their homes and to erect walls about the straggling little village. They changed its name to Halifax, in honour of the kindly English statesman, Lord Halifax, who was then President of the Lords of Trade.

The little settlement at Halifax was not left long in peace, for when the French saw that the English were strengthening themselves in Acadia they encouraged their friends, the Micmac Indians, to attack the settlement. This they did so stealthily and so persistently that at last Lord Cornwallis was forced to send out two companies of soldiers to scour the woods for Micmacs. No sooner were they driven away than a new danger menaced the little colony. This time it was an epidemic of fever, and for weeks it seemed that all the settlers would succumb to it. When, finally, they " weathered " the fever, small groups of them went to the French of Minas to buy cattle and sheep.

Each year new settlers came from England, but it was not until after the expulsion of the Acadians that Halifax was secure as a British settlement. After that many settlers came from New England and from Germany, and from then onwards Nova Scotia was secure as an English colony. So, from 1713, Nova Scotia has belonged to Britain, and she has therefore belonged to Britain longer than any other part of Canada.

20. THE TAKING OF CANADA

IT is the cloudy autumn night of September 12, 1759. Under cover of the darkness British boats, crowded with soldiers, are moving down the St. Lawrence. Their oars are muffled, and as they approach their landing-place there is not a sound to break the silence.

Suddenly a challenge rings out from a watchful sentry :

" Qui vive ? "

" La France," replies a Highland officer, who spoke French well, and had been told the French countersign. Thus the French sentry is satisfied, and in a few minutes the boats ground their keels in Foulon Cove, now known as Wolfe's Cove.

Wolfe was the first man ashore, followed quickly by twenty-four picked Highlanders. Their task was to seize the outpost on the brow of the cliff, which commanded the only way to the plain above. The cliff was steep and rocky, and it was a difficult feat for twenty-four men to climb it unseen and unheard by the sentries. Meantime the troops were landing on the beach. Wolfe was waiting in breathless suspense for news of his advance party. At last a British cheer rang through the darkness, and all knew the outpost had been surprised and captured.

Thus the narrow path to victory was laid open, and the troops poured up the steep ascent. Boat after boat brought more men and ammunition, and even guns. By dawn Wolfe had landed his army and drawn it up in battle array on the Plains of Abraham. There the French beheld them with amazement and dismay. Wolfe had already done what every one in Quebec believed impossible.

Montcalm, cool and courageous, rushed every available man to the spot. In close formation they advanced confidently to break the long thin line of British troops. It stood immovable, and made no reply to the French fire. Nearer and nearer came the French, firing vigorously and cheering, until they were within

THE CAPTURE OF QUEBEC

(From a drawing by Henry Sandham.)

forty paces. Then Wolfe gave the signal, and a volley crashed out from the British muskets. The front line of the French was almost wiped out. Then the British reloaded, advanced twenty paces, and so continued firing in volleys. Presently the French line broke under these smashing blows, and despite the bravery of Montcalm and his officers, it was impossible to rally their men. A charge by the British swept them from the field.

And so Wolfe had won Canada, though he did not live to see the completion of his success, for in the heat of battle he was shot in the breast. He struggled to go on, and when he could not he said to his attendant, " Do not let my men see me fall." When the first wild cheers of certain victory were filling the air, the great hero died.

His gallant foe, Montcalm, following his men in retreat, was shot almost at the same time as was Wolfe. " How long have I to live ? " he asked his surgeon, and when he was told not more than twelve hours, he said, " So much the better, for now I shall not see the surrender of my city."

A monument to the memory of the two leaders who died together now stands in the Public Gardens of Quebec, and on the battlefield there is a simple column which bears these words, " Here died Wolfe victorious."

21. THE AMERICAN WAR OF INDEPENDENCE

FIFTEEN years after Wolfe's victory at Quebec the American colonists became restless and dissatisfied with the way the British Government was treating them. Britain had been fighting wars all over the world, and fighting to defend these colonists from the French in Canada, but now, when she taxed her people in America to pay for these wars, they became very angry. " It is unfair," they said, " and against the laws of Britain. If we are to pay taxes we must be allowed to send members to Parliament."

King George III. would not hear of this, and when the colonists were told that the king would not allow them to be represented, they began to prepare for war. Even when the British Prime Minister, William Pitt, removed all taxes but that on tea, the colonists still objected. They formed themselves into an organization called " The Sons of Liberty," and every day young men drilled in preparation for war. Men were sent abroad to buy ammunition, and great supplies of food were gathered into store-houses in all the towns. Still the king would not allow the tax on tea to be withdrawn, and when a ship bearing a cargo of tea came into Boston harbour, a small group of the " Sons of Liberty," disguised as Indians, went on board and threw the tea into the water.

When King George heard of this he forbade any ships to go to Boston harbour to trade, and he ordered soldiers to be sent to the city to arrest the rebels. Then indeed the people of the city were very angry. Men began to gather on the field of Lexington, a few miles from Boston, and when the British troops arrived they found a small army waiting for them.

The British general did not allow his soldiers to begin battle at once. Instead, he ordered the American soldiers to disperse. When they would not, some one—it is not known on which side— fired a shot. Then the battle began in earnest. It was the first of many bitter struggles, for the war lasted until the year 1782.

THE FIGHT AT LEXINGTON.
(*C. Clark.*)

When the war began the revolutionists thought that they could take Canada easily. When Sir Guy Carleton, who was the governor of Canada, heard this, he laughed and said, " Let me tell you, Canada will have none of your disloyalty. The people are content and well satisfied with their laws."

It did not take the revolutionists long to discover the truth of his words. Their general, Richard Montgomery, with an army of three thousand men, succeeded in taking Montreal, but when he attempted to join his forces with those of Benedict Arnold, he met with dismal failure. On the last day of December 1775, Montgomery and Arnold opened their attack on the Canadian stronghold, Quebec. Montgomery began the battle before the Lower Town, but no sooner had he shouted to his men, " Come on, my brave boys, and Quebec is ours," than he found himself intercepted by British seamen and soldiers. In the struggle Montgomery was killed, and Benedict Arnold and his men were compelled to retreat.

Although the revolutionists failed to take Canada or to secure any assistance either from the French or English of Canada, they were successful in defeating the British army in their own country. So the British flag was taken down and the Stars and Stripes put in its place. The people no longer belonged to a British Colony. They were citizens of an independent country, which was called the United States of America.

22. THE UNITED EMPIRE LOYALISTS

MANY of the people in the American colonies would not fight against Great Britain during the American War of Independence. After the war the revolutionists, who thought that they should have fought, treated them very badly. Many of them had their homes burned and their property taken from them.

When Sir Guy Carleton, Governor of Canada, heard of their suffering, he invited them to come to Canada, where they received the honour of being called United Empire Loyalists. The British Government promised to give them farms in Canada, and to supply them with farm implements and with food for three years.

In the year 1783, and for five years afterwards, the Loyalists came pouring into Canada. Some of them came by ship to Nova Scotia and New Brunswick, and many others travelled hundreds of miles on horseback or on foot into what is now the Province of Ontario, and into the Eastern Townships of Quebec. In the first year of settlement over five thousand settled on farms near where the city of St. John, New Brunswick, now stands, and during the next ten years nearly all the counties of Ontario which border Lake Ontario were opened up. Indeed, the United Empire Loyalists made their way westward as far as what is now known as Brant county.

After their sufferings in the United States they were glad to be once more on British soil, but there were many times when they were discouraged and lonely, and longed for their old homes. The journey to Canada was but a beginning of their privations. Many of them had owned spacious, comfortable homes in New England, and now they had to live in humble log cabins, built by their own hands. Many had been wealthy merchants or owners of big plantations; now they had to clear the land, break new soil, and plant seed. Families had to live far from one another, and the " blazed " trail was the only road that led from one settlement to another.

LANDING OF THE LOYALISTS, 1783
(Henry Sandham.)

The year 1788 was a sad and pitiable year for the Loyalists in Ontario. It was called the " Hunger Year," for the crops failed, and the people who already had received food from the Government for three years had now to turn to hunting and fishing. The men of a settlement gathered week after week to go together into the forest to hunt deer and partridge. The women undertook to do the fishing, and the children went into the woods to gather berries and beech-nuts.

At last the dreadful winter days of the Hunger Year were over. Rich sap flowed in great abundance from the maples in the spring, and during the summer the grain grew with amazing rapidity. The people were so eager to taste food different from venison and the herbs they had been eating every day, that they gathered the green heads of barley and wheat and oats, and made porridge and biscuits. The crops which were harvested in the autumn were very plentiful, and never again did the Loyalists suffer such privations.

From that year they made great strides in progress. They extended their farms; they built new chimneys on their log cabins; and many of them were able to make extra pieces of furniture for their homes. So these brave people worked and struggled; they were kind and generous to one another and loyal to the new country that had given them a home. Many Canadians of to-day are descended from the United Empire Loyalists, and they are justly proud of their courageous, persevering ancestors.

23. CANADIAN PIONEERS

THE United Empire Loyalists were not the first English-speaking pioneers to come to Canada, for, as you will remember, two thousand people came to Halifax in the year 1749. Many people, too, settled in Quebec after the year 1763. The United Empire Loyalists, however, were among the first to settle in what is now New Brunswick, and to venture into Upper Canada. They were followed there in the first years of the nineteenth century by Lord Selkirk's first settlers, and a few years later he sent bands of Scottish people to break land and build homes on the banks of the Red River. At the same time that Lord Selkirk was trying to build up a new Scotland in the West,* the fiery Colonel Talbot was working diligently to found an Irish colony in what is now western Ontario. Hundreds of roads were " blazed " in the first years of the century, and crowds of people trekked along them to strange new homes.

The lot of the pioneers was a hard one, whether they settled in the Maritime Provinces, Quebec, Ontario, or the West. Many of them came to Canada from overcrowded mill towns in Great Britain. They had little or no experience of farming, and no knowledge of the desolation and loneliness of the new land. Their youth and vigour, combined with their determination to " make good," were their only assets.

How much they needed those assets ! Their task was not merely ploughing, seeding, harvesting. With cross-cut saws and axes they had to fell trees. With hand-ploughs and shovels they had to break the new land. But before one acre of land could be prepared for seed, cabins and stables had to be built.

The pioneers began their work before dawn, and they did not finish their daily tasks with the setting of the sun. If the pioneer woman had spent the day gathering berries, the evening must be passed in making driers. If the men had been gathering spoils

* See the Selkirk Settlers, page 62.

THE PIONEER.
(*Charles W. Jefferys.*)

from fur traps, the evening then must be spent in preparing skins for home tanning. Many winter evenings, as well as many winter days, were spent by the women in spinning and making clothing, either of cloth or of skins, and by the men in threshing grain with a flail, or in preserving the venison secured in the hunt. The problem of preserving meat was a difficult one, for it was impossible to secure salt. Fortunately the Indians came to their rescue with advice about smoking meats, and soon the smoke-house became a common addition to the little cluster of buildings on the pioneer farm.

But one must not think that the life of the pioneers was all work and no play. In the Maritime Provinces they had many " frolics," when the people of a settlement would gather at a farm and take part in a " barn-raising," followed usually by a merry dance. They also had chopping, ploughing, and occasionally threshing " frolics." In Upper Canada the " frolic " was called a " bee." The community gathering that was looked forward to with the most eagerness, however, was the " sugaring off." It came in the early spring when the sap of the maple was running, and was being boiled into syrup. The " taffy pull " was the attraction of " sugaring off," and it brought to the gathering not only the young farm people but throngs of hilarious " lumber jacks " and trappers.

Canadians of to-day owe a great deal to the early pioneers. It was they who blazed the trails and broke the land, who suffered hunger and loneliness, who planned, and struggled, and persevered. To-day, on our well-cultivated farms, in our prosperous towns, and in the justice of our government, we are enjoying the fruits of their indomitable courage.

24. CAPTAIN COOK AT NOOTKA SOUND

FOR years, indeed for centuries, men had been looking for a North-West Passage to China. Many Englishmen had led expeditions in search of it. Sir Martin Frobisher, Henry Davis, and Henry Hudson are but three who had made the attempt, and in the year 1776 Captain James Cook was sent out by the Admiralty on the same quest.

James Cook was the greatest navigator the British race has produced. He began life as a poor boy, and by his own exertions and ability he rose to be a captain in the Royal Navy. His first appearance in Canadian history was with Wolfe's expedition against Quebec. Cook was then the sailing master of one of the ships, and it was his task to find a safe passage for the fleet up the dangerous river.

He made valuable charts of the St. Lawrence, and at a later date a complete chart of the coast of Newfoundland. He discovered Australia and New Zealand, and his fame was at its height when the Government sent him to search for the North-West Passage.

In doing so Captain Cook took a different course from that followed by the other explorers. He sailed southward round the Cape of Good Hope, across the Indian Ocean, and thence into the Pacific to seek for the North-West Passage from that ocean. In March of 1778 he sighted that part of the coast of America which, nearly two hundred years before, Sir Francis Drake had named New Albion. Six weeks later he came to anchor in a sheltered cove on the coast of what is now British Columbia.

This cove was Nootka Sound, and as the Englishmen looked across it to the land, they marvelled at its strangeness. Here, instead of waving palms such as they had seen farther south, they saw gloomy forests of towering pine trees, and, beyond the forests, mountains covered with snow. As they looked, suddenly a birch-bark canoe, such as they had never seen before, came into view, and was paddled quickly to the side of their ship. While

[PLATE 24.

CAPTAIN COOK AT NOOTKA.
(*Charles W. Jefferys.*)

they wondered at the peculiar appearance of the tall, thin, dark-skinned occupants, more canoes appeared, until there were thirty-two in all, and they also approached their ships. At first the Englishmen were on their guard against these grim-faced natives, but when one man, evidently a chief, for he was dressed in rich furs, stood up in his canoe and made a speech, they knew the Indians wanted to be friendly and were inviting them to land. The white men, in turn, asked the Indians to come on board their ships.

Captain Cook and his men had to stay in Nootka Sound for four weeks while their ships, which had been tossed by violent storms, were made seaworthy. When at last they were ready to continue their voyage northward, the Indians brought them gifts of furs and skins, and begged them to return.

After leaving Nootka Sound, Captain Cook steered northward through the Pacific, round the coast of Alaska, until at last he came to Bering Strait. As he went up the coast he sent some men out in boats to take soundings, and other groups ashore to bring him reports of the land. He fell in with Russian traders, and they told him many tales of turbulent rivers, but they could tell him nothing of a passage that would lead him through the great wall of ice and snow. At last he turned back, convinced that there was no North-West Passage, but that the land of the whole Pacific was rich in fur-bearing animals, timber, and minerals. His reports to the Admiralty were the first ever made about the coast of what is now British Columbia, and for many years they were the only guides that other explorers had.

25. "FROM CANADA BY LAND"

WHEN Alexander Mackenzie was a little boy, living in Stornoway, on the Island of Lewis, he heard many tales of adventure in the Far West, for many Stornoway youths had become apprentices in the fur trade round Hudson Bay. No wonder, then, that Alexander, even before he was ten years old, decided that he would be an explorer.

He came to Montreal to live in 1778. At that time every one was talking of the achievements of the daring Captain Cook, and young Alexander resolved then that he would be as brave as that great seaman. Nor did he have many years to wait for an opportunity to prove his courage, for in 1785 he became a partner in a fur-trading company, and went to Fort Chipewyan, a distant post on Lake Athabaska.

Although the trade in furs was very profitable, Mackenzie longed to journey farther, for, he thought, " I can surely find a way across the mountains to the Pacific Ocean."

In 1789 he made a journey of twenty-eight hundred miles down the river which now bears his name, to the Arctic Ocean. Four years later Mackenzie set out to find the Western Sea. Before the snow became too heavy he and his little party of voyageurs reached the mouth of Smoky River. There they decided to build a fort and pass the winter.

Early the next spring, as soon as the ice had broken on the river, they continued their journey. What excitement there was when, eight days after they had left their winter quarters, they saw great mountain peaks looming before them !

But the days of happy eagerness were short, for they soon came to rapids, and there was danger of their canoes being battered to pieces by huge blocks of ice. Instead of continuing by water they had to cut a trail through the bush. When at last they were able to launch their canoes again the men had become weary and sick.

MACKENZIE AT THE PACIFIC BY THE OVERLAND ROUTE.
(Charles W. Jefferys.)

" No, I will not turn back.   We cannot be far from our goal,"
Mackenzie told his men when they begged him to give up the
expedition.

So all through the month of June, guided by friendly Indians,
they paddled up the Fraser River.   By July they had to leave their
canoes and struggle through underbrush and dense forest until
they came to the headwaters of the Bella Coola River.   Here the
friendly Indians gave them boats, and told them that the great
lake of salt water was within a few days' journey.

Once more the men were happy and eager.   On the morning
of the 20th of July they first began to feel the tang of salt air,
and two days later, from the cliffs above what is now called Burke
Channel, they looked out on the blue expanse of the Pacific.   Here,
on a great rock, Mackenzie inscribed these words : " Alexander
Mackenzie, from Canada by land, the twenty-second of July, one
thousand seven hundred and ninety-three, Lat. 52° 21' 48" N."

Thus Alexander Mackenzie realized his great ambition, and in
its attainment he won for himself an honoured place among our
early empire-builders.

26. THE JOURNEY OF SIMON FRASER

IN the year that Alexander Mackenzie began his journey overland to the Western Sea, another sturdy youth of a Scottish
family entered the service of the North-West Company.   He was
Simon Fraser, who, with his mother, a United Empire Loyalist,
had settled in Canada in the same year as Alexander Mackenzie
had come to Montreal.

Like Mackenzie, Simon Fraser was eager for adventure in the
Far West, and when promotion in the Company's service took
him to the fort on Lake Athabaska, he became more anxious than
ever to go beyond the mountains.   The opportunity came in 1805,
when he was given the important task of building the Company's
first fort west of the Rocky Mountains.

But this was not Simon Fraser's greatest achievement, for he
was soon to become famous as an explorer.   The members of
the North-West Company knew that Alexander Mackenzie had
gone down a great river until its rapids and rocks had become
so treacherous that he had been forced to cut a trail through the
bush.   They now asked Simon Fraser to follow this river to the
sea, for they hoped that, despite its rocks and rapids, it might make
a shorter route to the Pacific.

They had another reason, too, for wanting to find out all about
this river.   Two Americans had just discovered the mouth of the
Columbia River, and were laying claim to all the country west of
the Rockies, and many people in Canada, including several directors
of the Company, believed that the river which Mackenzie had
tried to go down was the Columbia.

Simon Fraser and his men had a hard time going down this
wild and dangerous river.   Sometimes they could pass whirlpools
only by climbing the steep rocks that rose on either side of the
foaming stream.   At other times they had to risk shooting the
rapids in their frail canoes.   At last, in the early summer of the
year 1808, after several of their canoes had been shattered, they

SIMON FRASER
(Charles W. Jefferys.)
By kind permission of the Canadian Bank of Commerce

entered calmer waters and paddled easily to the mouth of the river, which emptied into the Pacific. This, they found, was not the Columbia, as had been feared, but a mighty river which emptied into the Pacific some distance north of the Columbia.

But no sooner were they on the shores of the Pacific than a new difficulty arose. The Carrier Indians of the coast looked upon them with great anger and prepared to drive them away. At first Fraser could not understand their warlike spirit, for the Indians he had met on the journey had been friendly and helpful. Finally he found out that they were afraid of him and his men only because they thought the white men would be cruel to them and would take from them many of their treasures. After Fraser gave them gifts of tobacco, beads, and soap, and after they had heard stories of the daring adventures of the expedition, they rejoiced that these brave white men had come to their land.

Because Simon Fraser risked all the dangers of its whirlpools, rapids, and rocks, the river has ever since been known as the Fraser River. It became a great trade route of the West. The North-West Company, and, later, the Hudson's Bay Company, built forts along its banks, and the Indians, instead of trading with the Russians, brought their furs to the English trading-posts.

Thus Simon Fraser had a very important part in opening up the West for civilization and nation-building.

27. THE SELKIRK SETTLERS

In the early years of the nineteenth century many of the crofters of northern Scotland were driven from their farms. Lord Selkirk, a benevolent Scottish nobleman, was so distressed by their sufferings that he came to Canada to seek new homes for them. In Montreal he met a young Highlander, Colin Robertson, who had been in the service of the North-West Company at one of its western trading-posts. When Lord Selkirk told Robertson his purpose and asked his advice, he said, " My lord, take your people to the land at the forks of the Red and the Assiniboine rivers. There are no forests to be cleared away. The turning of a ploughshare will yield a crop. Cattle and horses can eat as they run. Some day, my lord, there will be a great empire extending far west from these two rivers."

After Alexander Mackenzie, the explorer, went to live in Scotland, he published his journal in which was recorded a graphic account of his western expedition. This book was much read and discussed, and Lord Selkirk had been one of its most interested readers. He had already sent groups of pioneers to Prince Edward Island, and to what is now eastern Ontario. He could send no more to the island because the land was all taken, and as the other colony had not grown in prosperity, he would not venture to extend it. Mackenzie's journal had given him an idea, and young Robertson's enthusiasm filled him with confidence. He would plant a colony of his countrymen at the forks of the Red and Assiniboine.

He bought many thousands of acres of land in the Red River District, and in the year 1811 he sent out a party of one hundred and twenty settlers. Although it was June when the little ships left Stornoway, they did not enter Hudson Bay and come to anchor before York Factory until late September.

Imagine the joy of the weary travellers when first they sighted land. Their pleasure was short-lived, however, for the governor

LANDING OF THE SELKIRK SETTLERS AT YORK FACTORY.
(*T. W. Mitchell.*)
By kind permission of Brigdens Ltd., Toronto.

of the fort refused to give them shelter as it was feared that there was some dread sickness among them. Moreover, the food stores at the fort were low, and he could give them very little.

Their leader, Miles MacDonell, was a man of great courage and resourcefulness, and he at once set them to work building log cabins for the winter. He made friends with the Indians, too, and persuaded them to bring the settlers buffalo meat and fish. So, although the new-comers must have found their surroundings very different from those at home, they were comfortable and fairly happy during their first winter in the new land.

In the spring they began their long walk to " the Land of Promise." By August they reached the forks of the Red and the Assiniboine, and selected the spot for their first settlement—a narrow tongue of land about a mile north of the Assiniboine. This land to-day is known as Point Douglas, and is within the city of Winnipeg.

After they laid out their farms and built their first homes they were driven from them by the Métis, or half-breed Indians, and had to seek shelter at the Hudson's Bay fort at Pembina. The next year they were joined by more settlers, and in the autumn of that year they had once more to go to Pembina. So followed many years of bitter struggle and hardship, years when crops were destroyed by locusts, floods, and heavy frosts. But the brave Scotsmen would not be beaten. They returned again and again and again, with unvanquished courage, determined to overcome every misfortune. To-day their perseverance has been rewarded, and the prophecy of Colin Robertson has been fulfilled, for a vast empire of prosperous farms and cities extends far west from the forks of the Red and the Assiniboine rivers.

28. WAR WITH THE UNITED STATES

TWENTY-NINE years after the American colonies had won their independence they declared war on Britain. The immediate cause of this war was Britain's announcement that she would not allow foreign ships to trade with Napoleon, because Napoleon, thinking himself master of Europe, had issued a decree that no nation should trade with Britain. But why, you ask, should the United States be interested in a struggle so far from her shores ? The reason was that the United States was carrying on a profitable trade with France, and after the declaration, when Britain seized American ships, the wrath of the American people knew no bounds.

Almost in a twinkling of an eye they gathered an army together and prepared to march into Canada. " We can take Canada without a shot, and without a soldier," one United States patriot said ; and another proclaimed, " All Canada is ready to throw off the yoke of Britain."

But " the yoke of Britain " was resting very lightly on the Canadian people, and under their able leader, Colonel Isaac Brock, they prepared not only to resist an American onslaught, but to make an attack against their enemy. This was a very daring thing for the Canadians to do, for they were poorly equipped in arms, and they had a population no greater than one-fifteenth of that of the United States. Nevertheless they forced Detroit to surrender, and so startled the confident Americans that they halted their raid into Canada.

In the autumn of 1812 the Americans suffered another defeat, this time at Queenston Heights. The Canadians sustained a bitter loss here, however, for their leader, Sir Isaac Brock, was killed just as the battle began.

There were many battles during the war, for the Americans sent three invading armies into Canada, and it would be impossible here even to name the victories of either side. The picture on the opposite page, however, brings to mind a victory slight in itself but very important in its effect.

" BURLINGTON RACES."
(Owen Staples, from a drawing by C. H. J. Snider.)
By kind permission of the John Ross Robertson Collection.

In April of the year 1813 the whole American fleet took part in a raid on York, now Toronto. Commander Sir James Yeo, of the British navy, was brought in haste from his base at Kingston, and for nearly the whole summer the two fleets played the game of cat and mouse on Lake Ontario. In heavy weather the American ships were almost useless, and Sir James Yeo watched for opportunities of making a " stormy " attack. Admiral Chauncey, on the other hand, desired to fight when light winds were blowing, and in September he thought his chance had come.

The British ships were at anchor in Humber Bay when the full American fleet hove in sight. The British fleet came out to give battle, and the two opposing forces were driven by the wind to Burlington. The American admiral endeavoured to drive the British ships on to the Burlington sands. Imagine his surprise when, just as he was expecting the British ships to ground on the sands, they were lifted over them by the high waves. Almost before Chauncey could realize what had happened, the British ships were riding securely on the waters of Burlington Bay. For a time the Americans hoped to keep the British ships in the Bay, but late in October Admiral Yeo very skilfully manœuvred them into the open waters of Lake Ontario, and without mishap took them to their base at Kingston.

The Burlington engagement can hardly be called a victory for the British, but it proved to the Americans that there was little hope of their securing control of Lake Ontario. Undaunted, however, during the winter they prepared for further naval battles, and it was not until the autumn of the next year that both warring nations were ready to make peace. Since that time the two countries have maintained a fine bond of friendship, a friendship so firm and so sincere that it is likely to withstand any threats of war.

29. THE COURAGE OF LAURA SECORD

ADVENTURES began to come to the little Laura Ingersoll when she was a tiny baby. In the year 1775 her parents brought her to Canada, for they were forced to flee from their home in Massachusetts because they were United Empire Loyalists. In the same year, and for the same reason, the Secord family sought refuge in Canada. When James Secord and Laura Ingersoll grew up they married and went to live near Queenston.

When Sir Isaac Brock called for recruits to join the Canadian army James Secord was one of the first to volunteer, and when General Brock fell on the battlefield at Queenston it was to the Secord home he was taken. On the same day James Secord was badly wounded, and he would have died had it not been for his brave wife, who found him on the field.

In the following year, however, the Americans were able to gain a footing in Canada, and early in June of that year, 1813, the Secords were forced to allow a number of American soldiers to be billeted in their home. One night Mrs. Secord heard them making plans. She heard the words " Fitzgibbon " and " Beaver Dams," and at once she was filled with dismay. Beaver Dams was a Canadian outpost some twenty miles away, and Lieutenant Fitzgibbon was the officer in charge. He had barely a hundred and fifty men under him, and when Mrs. Secord learned that the Americans were going to march against him next morning, she knew that she must warn Lieutenant Fitzgibbon, as her husband was not yet strong enough to go so far.

The first streaks of morning light were hardly showing in the sky when Mrs. Secord started out on her journey. She drove a cow before her as she went, and when the American sentry asked her where she was going she said she was driving the cow to the home of her sick brother at St. David's.

Once out of sight of the sentry she left the cow to pasture where it pleased, and hurried along the trail. But not for long was

"DRIVING A COW BEFORE HER, LAURA SECORD PASSED THE
AMERICAN SENTRIES."
(*J. R. Skelton.*)

she able to walk quickly and easily. The trail led through bush and swamps, and at one place she had to cross a stream by crawling along a log. Hour after hour she forced her way onward. At nightfall she came suddenly upon a group of Indians, and after she had controlled her fear she begged them to take her to Lieutenant Fitzgibbon.

They did so, and she gave her information at once, and he just as quickly dispatched messengers to Twelve Mile Creek for assistance. In the morning, when the enemy made their attack, they found themselves surrounded by British soldiers and Indians, and were compelled to surrender.

Laura Secord lived for over fifty years after her adventurous journey, and during that time many people visited her at her home in Chippawa to hear from her own lips the story of her great achievement. In the year 1860 King Edward VII., who was then Prince of Wales, went to see her, and later he sent her a gift of five hundred dollars.

When Laura Secord died a monument was erected in her honour at Queenston Heights. On it these words were written: " This monument has been erected by the Government of Canada to Laura Ingersoll Secord, who saved her husband's life in the battle on the Heights on October 13, 1812, and who risked her own in conveying to Captain Fitzgibbon information by which he won the battle of Beaver Dams, January 24, 1813."

30. TRAVEL BY CART AND CANOE

THE Selkirk settlers went to their new homes at the forks of the Red and Assiniboine rivers on foot, and each winter for several years they returned on foot to Pembina. But before the year 1820 they had constructed vehicles, both for the trail and for the rivers.

The carts which they made have become famous as the " Red River Carts," and twice a year a brigade of them went creaking down the trail to St. Paul. They were sturdy two-wheeled wagons built entirely of wood. Even the pegs that held the spokes in place and that fastened the box to the frame were of wood. When a cart broke down the driver found all he needed for repairing it in the nearest bush. These carts were remarkably strong, for they could carry in their light frame boxes a cargo weighing well over half a ton. Built entirely of wood, we say, but we should add that the wooden wedges were strengthened by heavy " shagganappi " strapping. This " shagganappi " was made of tanned ox-hide, and a driver never risked going on a journey without a substantial roll of it in his cart.

Nor were the trips to St. Paul the most important cart journeys of the year. Every buffalo hunt was followed by a great throng of carts sent out to bring in the spoils. The signal of the return from the hunt was the shrill, constant creaking of the carts, a sound which was listened for in every settlement, and which was followed always by celebrations and rejoicing.

The settlers, living as they were on river banks, had need for boats. The birch-bark craft of the voyageur was too fragile for their needs, so they hollowed out large tree trunks and shaped them like canoes. These boats were as strong as the carts, and like the carts they had a very important part in the buffalo hunt, for in them spoils were sometimes carried to the encampment and frequently to distant settlements. " York boats," strongly built, were introduced by Governor Simpson of the Hudson's Bay

THE GOVERNOR OF RED RIVER TRAVELLING BY CANOE
(*E. J. Dinsmore, after an old print.*)

Company. These were rowed by eight men, and could carry three or four tons.

Every June flotillas of boats, manned as a rule by French-Canadians in the employ of the Hudson's Bay Company, set out to carry the settlers' surplus produce to one of the Company's forts. By 1821 Norway House had become the chief centre of this trade, and there, in late June, a great throng of traders assembled, not only the Frenchmen with their boats full of farm produce, but the voyageurs from the north with their birch-bark canoes loaded with furs. Then a great market began, and usually, after days of trading, the voyageurs returned to their northern posts, and the Frenchmen continued on their way to York Factory, this time with cargoes of furs. In the early autumn or late summer they returned to the settlements, carrying mails and winter supplies of clothing for the settlers.

For more than half a century the Red River cart and the canoe played an important part in the opening up of the West. By cart and canoe settlers sought out new homes; by the same means missionaries went to their far western parishes, and Company officials surveyed the country and endeavoured to keep order and administer justice. Indeed there are many pioneers in the West to-day who first went to their land by cart and canoe, and among their most thrilling reminiscences are their accounts of those first journeys.

31. TRAVEL BY STAGE-COACH

" HE who has been once to church and twice to the mill is a traveller," was a saying in Upper Canada little more than a hundred years ago. And a traveller he was indeed, for such journeys could be made only on foot along a narrow path through the forest. Later the path was widened to a trail for pack or saddle horses, and about the year 1816 " corduroy " roads were built for the passage of stage-coaches and carrioles.

Queer as the " corduroy " roads would seem to-day, they were nevertheless strong and secure. Their security, in fact, grew with their use, for the logs, laid crosswise in the road, were sunk into the ground by traffic, and formed an enduring foundation—so enduring, indeed, that corduroy roads are still in existence. Upon these roads carrioles, calèches, and lumber-wagons carried the early pioneers to their new homes, to market, and to meeting-places, and it was over these roads that the first stage-coaches in Upper Canada made their journeys.

Would you like to journey by stage-coach? Then let us pretend that it is the year 1817, and that we are travelling from Montreal to Kingston. Before five o'clock in the morning we are at the post-house, and have our luggage piled on the back of the stage, and ourselves, wrapped in buffalo robes, seated within. On the tick of the hour four spanking horses are hitched to the stage, and we are off. The horses prance along at a good speed, for the driver has instructions to drive six miles an hour, and by half-past six we are in Lachine.

Now we must decide whether we shall continue by coach or go to the Cascades by boat.—By boat? Very well, then. We must find a place, and, with our robes wrapped about us and cushions at our backs, we sail to the Cascades. There we change again to the stage, and at Côteau we transfer to the boat for the sail to Cornwall. So we journey on for nearly ten days, sometimes gliding in a smooth-running bateau, and sometimes jolting wearily in a stage-coach.

A CANADIAN STAGE-COACH IN WINTER.
(E. J. Dinsmore, after an old print.)

Our journey by coach is not without events. Sometimes, when the pull uphill is too much for the horses, we must walk. Several times we have to wait while the oxen of a near-by farmer pull our coach out of a ditch. And perhaps, but only perhaps, for it did not happen often, we may have an alarming adventure, for a highwayman may dash into the road suddenly and command the driver to stop the coach and all the passengers to give him their money. Adventure or no adventure, though, by the time we reach the next post-house we are as glad as the horses and their driver, for at each post-house there is time to rest and to have something to eat.

At last we are in Kingston. Shall we continue our journey to York? We can, for in this very year a coach road has been opened up. The man of the post-house tells us that the road is good, for several bridges have been built and a gravel road has been made for part of the distance. We should make the journey in four days, or even less, but perhaps we would rather not risk any more weary travelling. Perhaps we are tired of being pioneers in the early years of the last century, and would prefer to hurry to Toronto from Kingston in a few hours either by train or in an automobile.

Before we decide, let us look at the stage-coach in our illustration. It seems comfortable, does it not? Can you get a glimpse within? The seats are deep and have cushions. If we are making our journey in the winter, we shall have blocks of heated hardwood at our feet and a heavy buffalo robe wrapped about our knees. "A journey like that in winter!" you exclaim. You need not fear it, for the coach and horses skim along at great speed. There is no danger of being delayed by " heavy " muddy roads, and if a snowstorm should stay our progress we can take a turn at shovelling snow with the driver and the farmers who will come to our aid.

32. TRAVEL BY STEAMSHIP

A JOURNEY in Canada in the year 1800 could not be undertaken after the hasty packing of a travelling bag and the purchase of a railway ticket. It was necessary then to travel almost entirely by water, and for days before the voyage the prospective traveller was busy getting ready his tent, his buffalo robes, pillows, cooking utensils, and food, and even when these were all in readiness he might be delayed for many days, for no boat sailed alone. They went in brigades, and not until a brigade was assembled could the traveller begin his journey. If he were travelling from Montreal to York (Toronto) he might, in fair weather, hope to arrive at his destination in ten days. But lucky was the traveller who escaped storms, heavy currents, and tiresome portaging over rapids !

By the year 1809 changes were being made in river and lake travel, for in that year a company in Montreal built a small steamer called the *Accommodation*, and, seven years later, a steamship seven times as large was running on Lake Ontario. This ship, the *Frontenac*, which is shown in the illustration, was the first steamer to travel on the waters of the Great Lakes, and her launching at Ernesttown, on the Bay of Quinte, was an occasion of great rejoicing. The *Kingston Gazette* at the time described the event in these words, " She descended with majestic grandeur into her proper element, the admiration of a great throng of spectators. . . . Good judges have proclaimed her to be the best piece of naval architecture yet produced in America."

Would you like to imagine that you are travelling in Canada a hundred years ago ? First you must decide whether you are rich enough to travel on the ship itself, or whether you may have a place in the little boat which is towed by the steamer. If you are a new settler, lately arrived in the country, your slender purse may let you have no more than sitting space on the " trailer " boat. But do not mind this ; " trailer " or not, the steamship makes its way quickly up the lake, and in four days, if all goes well,

AN EARLY CANADIAN STEAMSHIP.
By kind permission of Rous and Mann, Toronto.

you will be in York. But everything may not go well. The ship will have to stop frequently to take on wood, and if it should happen that the pile of wood falls short of sixty cords you can do nothing but wait for it to be replenished.

By the year 1850 water travel in Canada had improved greatly. Then, if you were going on a journey, you could travel in a steamship like the one in the illustration, which was as luxurious as any ship sailing in the waters of Europe. You could have a cabin and a chair on the deck, and your meals cooked for you and served in a dining-room. And, what is more important, you could come from Montreal to York in two days, and without delay you could continue to Niagara.

If you wanted to travel by steamer, you would have to do it either in the late spring, the summer, or the early autumn. With the first frosts of autumn the ships required more wood, and consequently journeys were delayed by many stops. By November the lake was frozen over, and not until the ice melted in spring was it safe to undertake a voyage.

It is no wonder, then, that the people of Canada, although they were well satisfied with the comforts and the speed of the lake steamers during the season, were anxious to have railways by which they might travel and ship their products all the year round.

Although the railway was invented before the steamship it was the latter which came into use first in Canada. One reason for this is obvious : the steamer could be built and launched at a much less cost than the path of a railway could be cut through the heavily-wooded land. Early visitors to Canada from England marvelled at the luxury of Canadian ships. Sir Richard Bonnycastle recorded in his book, *The Canadas*, that they had as many conveniences as fashionable hotels, and that "they are fitted out with a service of plate and china. They very often have music on board, and in the ladies' cabin a piano." Visitors were equally amazed at the number of steamers that plied on the rivers, carrying produce, especially lumber, from town to town. In one diary of an early pioneer it was recorded that steamers entered or departed from the harbours of many towns " almost hourly."

33. THE FIRST RAILWAY IN CANADA

On a certain night of early summer in the year 1837 every one in the little village of La Prairie was greatly excited, for on that night the *Kitten* was to make its first journey from La Prairie, on the St. Lawrence, to St. Johns, on the Richelieu River.

"As soon as the moon is out," the people whispered to one another, but the moon came out and the *Kitten* did not move. The engine chugged two or three times, then grumbled lazily and was silent. The engineer who had brought the *Kitten* from England became angry and impatient, but do what he would he could not make the engine do more than "meow." So the next morning the train went on its old way, drawn by horses, to St. Johns, and for many mornings thereafter the horses had to draw the train either from La Prairie or from St. Johns.

At last the directors agreed to give the *Kitten* another chance. The fire-box was well "stoked" with wood, and the tank filled with water. The fire was not allowed to burn low for a moment. Then the throttle was opened, and to the amazement of the crowd, and the relief of the directors, the *Kitten* moved forward. Nor did she stop after her first "chug"; instead, she moved faster and faster, until in a few minutes she was gambolling along at a steady rate of twenty miles an hour.

Once the experiment of the *Kitten* had proven a success other railways of greater length were built. "If a train can go sixteen miles by steam surely it can go a hundred and sixteen," every one agreed, and in less than ten years there were dozens of railway companies formed in Canada, and almost an equal number of lines either being surveyed or built.

The building alone meant a boon to Canadian industry, for lumbermen along the lines of the proposed railways were busy getting out rails, and crews of workmen were engaged in laying them and topping them with flat bars of iron. Indeed, for over thirty years there was hardly a person in Canada who was not

THE FIRST CANADIAN RAILWAY.
(E. J. Dinsmore.)

interested in the progress of railway building. Far-sighted statesmen had visions of the country's growth to empire size, and enterprising men of business saw commerce and profit far outstripping anything ever before seen or dreamed of.

But despite enthusiasm, propaganda, and work, the railways of Canada progressed slowly. The second railway to be opened up, instead of being longer, was only eight miles in length, and ran around the rapids between Montreal and Lachine. The first railway in Upper Canada exceeded all the others in length, but it had a sadder fate than the *Kitten*, for its engine could not be persuaded to mount a high grade near Queenston, and for nine years horse-cars were used on it.

These lines were "portage" railways; that is to say, they followed the track of a "portage" connecting two stages of water transport. In time the railway was to act as an independent carrier, competing directly with the water-routes, but the enterprise of railway building developed very slowly, partly because the steamship gave good service and partly because, at this time, Canada was in the midst of bitter political conflict. It was not until after the winning of Responsible Government, about which you will read on page 80, that the railway builders began in earnest to extend their lines long distances.

This is but the first of the story of railway building in Canada. It has been made up of many failures but also of many great successes, and the visions of both statesmen and men of business were realized long before the close of the century.

34. THE MAIL

WHEN Canada was a very young country, people had little means of sending messages. Very rich people living in Quebec or Montreal sent private messengers from one place or the other to carry packets of letters to their friends. Sometimes people were lucky enough to persuade the Government courier to carry letters for them, and in spring, when the hunters returned to Three Rivers, Montreal, or Quebec, they also distributed news. Indeed, their home-coming was an event of great importance, if for no other reason than that they could give news of the settlers whom they had seen along their way, and could deliver messages entrusted to them.

In the year 1721, only five years before Pierre La Vérendrye went to his lonely fort on Lake Nipigon, a regular mail service was begun from Quebec to Montreal. During the spring, summer, and autumn people could have news from their friends in either city about once a fortnight. During the winter, although the service was carried on by couriers, it was never certain that messages would reach their destination, for the courier might be storm-bound in a settler's home; he might be captured and held by unfriendly Indians, or he might, if he were filled with a desire for adventure, join a group of *coureurs de bois* and go to the western fur country.

When Canada became British in 1763, the postal service of the thirteen colonies was extended to Canada by its organizer, Benjamin Franklin, and post-offices were opened at Quebec, Montreal, and Three Rivers. At intervals of nine miles post-houses were opened along the road, and habitants were put in charge of them. Here mail couriers, whether they were travelling on horseback with the mail fastened in heavy leather saddle-bags, or were making their journey luxuriously in a post-chaise, stopped to rest, to leave mail, and to add mail to their bags.

At the same time that Franklin organized his Canadian mail

EARLY CANADIAN POSTAL DELIVERY
(*A. Sherriff Scott.*)
By kind permission of the Dominion Archives, Ottawa

service he also began a Canada-Atlantic service, and every week couriers went from Montreal to New York with mail.

When the American War of Independence broke out the service was discontinued, and Canada's only possible way of getting mail to a port was by sending it to Halifax. The Montreal-Halifax service was dangerous and tedious. The couriers had to travel over little-known and poorly-blazed trails. The journey took them over seven weeks, and very often the courier had to travel by night in order to complete it in that time.

After the United Empire Loyalists came to Upper Canada post-offices were opened at Kingston, York (Toronto), Hamilton, Niagara, and Amherstburg. During the open season the mail was carried in sailing vessels, but during the winter the courier went from post-house to post-house on snowshoes, or if he had the good fortune to have a route over a trail that was sometimes " broken " by settlers, he went on horseback. The courier did not make regular nine-mile stops, but anchored his little boat, or stopped his horse, or loosened his snowshoes, at every settlement. He left a packet of mail with a citizen, who acted as post-master. His parting instructions to the " master " were, " Have your mail ready for me when I return, for I cannot wait. I must ' fly ' to catch the ship's courier, you know."

The citizen to whom the mail was entrusted usually chose the most convenient means of distributing it. He might take it to the settlement mill or store, and on many occasions he took it with him to church on Sunday morning. Such an incident is illustrated in our picture.

With our very efficient, regular and fast air mail service to-day, we cannot but realize how far we have progressed beyond these early days in Canada.

35. TROUBLE IN LOWER CANADA

EARLY days in Canada were stormy days indeed. No sooner was the country safe from an invading army than political rights became a subject of argument and bitterness. In both Upper and Lower Canada there was enmity between the Legislative Council and the House of Assembly, for the Council had full control of all money matters, and it could cancel every Act of the House of Assembly. The members of the Assembly were, for the most part, the representatives of the common people, and the members of the Council belonged to the wealthy group of citizens. In Lower Canada there was the added difficulty that the members of the Council belonged to the English-speaking citizens, while the Legislative Assembly was made up of representatives of the French people.

Although the British Government tried to satisfy the demands of both sections of the people, ill-will grew to bitter hatred. In Upper Canada the leader of the people who were ready to fight for their rights was William Lyon Mackenzie; the leader in Lower Canada was Louis Joseph Papineau.

Louis Joseph Papineau was a powerful orator. His voice, beautiful and eloquent, filled the people with loyalty to him, and likewise with the spirit of rebellion. In October of the year 1837, when he went to address a meeting of *Patriotes* at St. Charles, he found the people ready for battle. They had erected a wooden pillar, and on it they had placed a cap of liberty—the red Phrygian cap which was the badge of popular rights in the French Revolution. When Papineau stood before it the crowd burst into lusty cheers. After he had spoken to them they marched around the pillar singing patriotic songs, and each man in turn placed his hand on the pillar and took an oath " to be faithful to the cause of his country, and to conquer or die for her." Before the meeting ended one of Papineau's ardent lieutenants, Wolfred Nelson, shouted, " The time has come to melt our spoons into bullets."

A POLITICAL MEETING IN LOWER CANADA.
(*Fergus Kyle.*)

These were the words that lit the powder of rebellion, and in less than two weeks *Patriotes* all over Lower Canada were arming themselves for battle. The first open conflict in Lower Canada so fired the enthusiasm of the rebels in Upper Canada that they, too, began drilling and gathering arms. Mackenzie was as fiery a leader as Papineau and as certain of success. Like Papineau, too, his ambition was to proclaim Canada a republic. His plan was to capture Toronto without delay and, with that as his stronghold, to extend his campaign throughout Upper Canada. But in his impetuous enthusiasm Mackenzie overestimated the strength of his followers.

By December of 1837 the battle in Upper Canada had been fought and lost, but all through the winter and the next summer trouble brewed and broke out in Lower Canada. In the end many of the leaders of the rebellion were forced to flee, among them Louis Joseph Papineau, who lived for several years in Paris. When he returned he was made a member of the Canadian parliament, and had some part in putting into effect the new laws which were made to remove the causes of the rebellion.

Like Papineau, Mackenzie had to flee to a foreign country for safety. He went to the United States and did not return to Canada until after Responsible Government had been granted. In 1851 he was elected to the Legislative Assembly, but as there was no need to fight any further battle for the people's rights, he found himself strangely uncomfortable in the House, and in a few years he resigned his seat.

36. THE WINNING OF RESPONSIBLE GOVERNMENT

WHEN the Home Government heard of the rebellion they sent Lord Durham to Canada to find out the real causes of the trouble. After six months he made a report to the queen, and in a very short time the Act of Union was passed. By this Act Upper and Lower Canada were united under one governor and one parliament ; the people were given the right to elect the councillors who advised the governor, and all matters relating to money were entrusted to the people's representatives, the members of the Assembly.

Now these were the very things the rebels had been fighting for, but there were many people in Canada on the opposite side who were determined that the new laws should not be carried out. " We shall have Responsible Government—not a hair's breadth less," the leaders of the reformers said, and in 1848 Lord Elgin, who was governor, put the Act of Union into force.

One of the first bills to be brought up in the new parliament was the Rebellion Losses Bill. By it people in Lower Canada whose property had been destroyed during the rebellion were to be paid for their losses. People in Upper Canada had already been paid, and it was only fair that citizens of Lower Canada should be compensated too.

" Paying traitors ! Paying traitors ! " became the cry of the Tories who were opposed to the bill, and on the day that it passed the two houses of parliament they broke out in rebellious anger.

Had you been in Montreal on that day, April 25, 1849, you would have seen a strange sight. A carriage driven by prancing horses came dashing away from the parliament buildings, and as it rushed through the streets a shower of eggs and other things was thrown at it. But why, you ask ? Because Lord Elgin, the governor, was riding in that carriage, and the " young bloods " of the Tory party were taking this way of showing how angry they were with him.

[PLATE 36.

THE BURNING OF THE PARLIAMENT BUILDINGS, MONTREAL, 1849.
(*From a contemporary print by E. Hides.*)

They did not vent the full force of their anger in egg-throwing alone, for that night a mob of Tory leaders surged into the Assembly meeting and drove the members from their seats. One angry youth of the party took the Speaker's chair, and from it he issued commands for the breaking of furniture and burning of papers. In the midst of this anger and destruction a fire broke out, and in a few minutes Tories and Reformers were working together to quell the flames. The parliament buildings were completely destroyed, and Montreal was never again the seat of provincial or national government.

Thus Responsible Government had a stormy reception in Canada, but since then Canadians have learned that it is one of the dearest treasures of democratic rule. The names of the two men who worked with Lord Elgin to bring it about, Robert Baldwin and Louis La Fontaine, have honoured places among those of our country's greatest statesmen.

While the people of Canada were struggling, some to secure Responsible Government, and others to prevent its establishment, a similar battle was being waged in Nova Scotia, New Brunswick, and Prince Edward Island. They did not resort to battle and fiery rioting in these provinces, but their campaign was no less vigorous. In New Brunswick the advocate for Responsible Government was Lemuel Wilmot, and by his brilliant speeches and newspaper articles he was able to win the support of the people. In Nova Scotia the cause of Responsible Government was sponsored by a clever young man, Joseph Howe, who through his paper, the *Nova Scotian*, first began his campaign against the Tories. Although Howe had to carry on his campaign for over ten years before he won, he at last had the satisfaction of seeing Responsible Government established in Nova Scotia.

37. THE COMING OF NEW CANADIANS

THIS picture is especially interesting because it was made by the artist on the spot. The people and the scene are shown as he actually saw them at the time. Only twenty-two years had elapsed since the opening of the first Canadian railway (1837), shown on page 74, and here we see trains and locomotives in the railway station at Toronto. Although thirty more years were to pass before Canada had a railway from coast to coast, many hundreds of miles had already been constructed. As yet, however, they belonged to separate and unconnected systems.

There was, for example, a railway from Halifax to Windsor and Truro, and another from St. John to Moncton, but there was no connection between the two. In Quebec lines ran from Montreal to Portland, Maine, with a branch to Levis. The first railway bridge over the St. Lawrence had just been completed at Montreal, and the line to Toronto had been open for three years. Beyond Toronto one could go by train as far as Buffalo, Sarnia, Goderich, or Collingwood. There were no Canadian railways at all west of the great lakes.

Of course the trains were nothing like so good as they are to-day. In fact we should find them most uncomfortable. The coaches, as we can see, were small, and were built of wood. They were heated only by box stoves. The locomotives burnt wood, and lots of it. The brakes were weak and the road-bed uneven, and so the jolting and bumping was terrible. Nevertheless every one was very pleased and enthusiastic, and more and more lines were being built as fast as the money could be found.

The family group having a meal on the platform are immigrants who have just arrived from the Old Country. Thousands of them were coming in every year, and they mostly settled in Ontario, or Canada West, as it was then called. A good many found work in Quebec, and some came direct by sea to the Maritime Provinces. Settlement on the prairie had scarcely begun, and British Columbia had only just received the first big rush of gold-miners.

IMMIGRANTS AT A RAILWAY STATION, TORONTO.
(From a contemporary drawing by W. Armstrong.)

The immigrants we see in the picture probably came to Quebec by sailing ship, and the voyage might take four or five weeks. The ships were crowded, and the accommodation very rough. The immigrants had to provide their own bedding, utensils, and food. They prepared their own meals, and the box that served as their pantry was also their dining-table. But in spite of all hardships and discomforts they arrived full of hope and determination. Those in the picture certainly look as though they would make the best of things in their new surroundings.

The children may have been frightened by the Indian woman who, you see, is selling souvenirs, but it is more than likely that they have made friends with her. The father, perhaps, is anxious to know how they are to journey from Toronto. Will they go by steam train or horse train, or will the schooner that is now sailing across the bay be able to carry them? It is possible, but it depends on what part of Canada West they are going to; they may have to journey in an ox-cart. And what of the mother? She looks pleased, and perhaps it is because the man has told her that he has just learned that mail is distributed much more quickly in Canada than ever before—for now it is carried on steamships and as far as possible on the railway. Perhaps, and the thought fills her with happiness, there will very soon be letters for them from their old home in England, Scotland, or Ireland.

Immigration has had its ups and downs, influenced mainly by general conditions. As transportation facilities have expanded and improved and the various parts of the world have been drawn together more closely, new citizens have come to our Dominion from all corners of the globe.

38. THE FIRST TRANSATLANTIC CABLE

FOR us to-day, who can telephone or telegraph to the most distant parts of the earth, it is difficult to realize how slow communication was only seventy years ago. It took four or five weeks to send a letter from Canada to England, and there was no other method of communication.

The invention of the electric telegraph had speeded things up slightly, and a telegraph line from Quebec to Toronto, built in 1845, enabled important news to reach central Canada a few days sooner than by mail. Other telegraph lines were put up, and there was always one where there was a railway, as it was necessary for the control of the trains.

No sooner was the land telegraph a commercial success than inventors began to seek some means of telegraphing across the ocean. The main difficulty was that a bare wire would allow the electric current to escape into the water, and so it was necessary to enclose the wire in something that would keep in the current and protect the wire. In a few years the right substance had been found, and some short submarine cables were in operation. The first was between Dover in England and Calais in France, and the first in North America connected Prince Edward Island with New Brunswick. Then Ireland was linked by cable to England, and Newfoundland to Nova Scotia.

The next step was to lay a cable across the Atlantic, and so put the New World into instant communication with the Old. But this was a very different proposition from the short cables already in existence, and many people who ought to have known better said it was impossible. It was believed that the distance alone (1,300 miles) would make it impossible to send electric signals. Some said that the Atlantic was too deep for the cable to sink to the bottom, and if it did the weight of water would prevent the sending of messages. There were all kinds of other and more real difficulties, but the engineers were sure they could

LANDING THE ATLANTIC CABLE AT HEART'S CONTENT.

(From a contemporary drawing.)

be overcome. So at last the Atlantic Telegraph Company was formed, the money subscribed, and the first attempt made in the year 1856. It failed, and the scoffers shouted, " We told you so." But the engineers tried again, and in 1858 the first message came through : " Europe and America are united by telegraphy. Glory to God in the highest, and on earth peace, goodwill toward men."

There were great rejoicings on both sides of the Atlantic at this wonderful achievement, but they were short lived. Through ignorance of the nature of electricity the current used was too powerful and destroyed the insulating cover. The cable was useless, and millions of dollars had been lost.

It was seven years before more money could be raised to make another attempt. Just then the *Great Eastern*, the largest ship afloat, was launched, and she was commissioned to lay the cable. Again the cable broke as it was being laid, but a second attempt was successful, and in July 1866 the western end of the cable was landed at Heart's Content, Newfoundland.

Thus the engineers, by perseverance and ingenuity, had overcome heart-breaking disappointments. The cable worked, and was a complete success. Others quickly followed, and there are now fifteen crossing the Atlantic, and many others connecting every continent of the globe.

Even while they were being laid a Scottish scientist, Clerk Maxwell, was busy with the experiments that led the way for Signor Marconi to show how messages could be sent without wires.

39. THE DOMINION OF CANADA

AFTER the rebellion of 1837, Upper and Lower Canada were united under one parliament, but in a few years the people became dissatisfied with this form of government. One reason for their wanting a change was that very often questions which were of importance to one province were settled by a majority from the other province. Another reason for dissatisfaction was that Upper Canada had no more members in the house of parliament than Lower Canada, although it had many more people. " Representation by population " became the slogan of the political leaders in Upper Canada, and it became the terror of all the people in Lower Canada, for they feared that, if Upper Canada were given more representatives, they would be controlled entirely by the upper province.

While the political leaders of Canada, John A. Macdonald, Sir Etienne Taché, and George Brown, were discussing what could be done to improve the government of Canada, word came from the Maritime Provinces that the people there were having similar difficulties. It was decided, therefore, that representatives of Canada should meet with representatives of the Maritime Provinces to discuss the possibilities of confederation. This first meeting, held in Charlottetown, was so successful that it was decided to hold a second one in Quebec in a year's time. After the meeting in Quebec in 1864, Canadian statesmen were agreed that all the British provinces in America should be joined together in a federation—that is, that all the provinces should have one house of parliament, which would decide questions of interest to the whole country. Each province, too, should have a Legislative Assembly, which would deal with matters of interest only to that province.

After the meeting at Quebec the leaders went through the country explaining to the people the great change that was about to take place. Several statesmen went to England to ask the consent of the British Government. When this was granted, the

CONFEDERATION DAY.
(*E. J. Dinsmore.*)

British North America Act was passed, and with its passing the Dominion of Canada came into being. The Act was passed on July 1, 1867, and for that reason the 1st of July is called " Dominion Day." The illustration here is of the first Dominion Day Celebration held in Ottawa before the newly-erected parliament buildings. Sir John A. Macdonald, who with his great political opponent, George Brown, had worked very diligently to bring about Confederation, was made the first premier of the Dominion.

At first only four provinces came into the confederation : Quebec, Ontario, Nova Scotia, and New Brunswick. In 1870 Manitoba became a province of the Dominion ; in 1871 British Columbia joined the Dominion, and three years later Prince Edward Island. In 1905 the two new provinces of Saskatchewan and Alberta were added.

In 1869 Newfoundland rejected an invitation to become part of the Dominion of Canada, and although union was mooted again later, it was not until 1949 that this proud British colony officially became the tenth province of Canada.

The names of the members of the first Dominion Ministry are worthy of inclusion here, for they were men who will always be considered among Canada's greatest statesmen—John A. Macdonald, Prime Minister and Minister of Justice ; George E. Cartier, Militia and Defence ; S. Leonard Tilley, Customs ; Alexander T. Galt, Finance ; William McDougall, Public Works ; William P. Howland, Inland Revenue ; Adams G. Archibald, Secretary of State for the Provinces ; A. J. Ferguson Blair, President of the Privy Council ; Peter Mitchell, Marine and Fisheries ; Alexander Campbell, Postmaster-General ; Jean C. Chapais, Agriculture ; Hector L. Langevin, Secretary of State for Canada ; and Edward Kenny, Receiver-General.

40. A GROWING PEOPLE

DURING the seventy years that elapsed between the coming of the Loyalists and the movement for confederation there were many great changes made in Canada. The people in the Canadas and in the Maritime Provinces won reforms in government. New Brunswick came into being during that time, and settlers from all parts of Great Britain opened up new sections of land.

Nowhere were these changes more conspicuous than in Upper Canada. The pioneer's log cabin was enlarged, or replaced by a substantial house of brick, frame, or stone. His heavy burden of work was lightened by the introduction of farm implements. During the years between 1815 and 1840 the population of Ontario was nearly doubled, and with this rapid growth the tiny villages built on the edge of the forest became prosperous towns. Stores were opened ; the weaver and the blacksmith and even the cabinet-maker found employment. In a few years the wagon-maker, one of the first mechanics to prosper by these changing conditions, was able to build a factory, and the industry rapidly became established in all the leading towns. Another sign of prosperity was the fact that the work of making men's suits was taken from the home and put into the hands of a tailor.

The towns of Upper Canada grew very rapidly. The post-office and the shipping warehouse followed the churches, and after these came schools. Stores increased in number, and the old gloomy rooms, packed with a queer assortment of supplies, began to be improved with " fronts " and displays. The community hall did not come until later, but during this time the town stores served the same purpose, and at least once a week they were thronged with eager buyers.

During the first years of this prosperity the town-dwellers were only those engaged in industry and trade. In a few years prosperous farmers began to retire to the towns, and their substantial houses aided the towns' growth. The town of our

MAIN STREET, PICTON, ONTARIO, 1869.
(*George Ackermann.*)
By kind permission of the John Ross Robertson Collection.

illustration is Picton, a small town of central Ontario. The drawing was made on the spot, and shows the people and the buildings as they were in the year 1869. The red-brick houses were among the first of the kind to be built in Ontario.

Although the growth of the towns in Upper Canada was due at first to the increased population and the new markets opened up by the improvement in shipping, there was another cause of almost equal importance. During these years, and for many years afterwards, lumbering was done on a large scale. The towns in the vicinity of the Picton of our illustration had large lumber-yards, sawmills, planing-mills, and furniture factories. Every spring great river drives came into Trenton and Belleville, and into all the towns on the Lake Ontario water-front.

Political unrest and the demand for change grew apace with the towns. Stirring political meetings were held regularly, and drew great crowds. At Adolphustown, a few miles from Picton, twenty years before, there had been a young law apprentice who had the gift of leadership. His name was John Alexander Macdonald, and in those early days he gave many fiery addresses in the community. He so won the hearts of the people that when he entered provincial politics they were ready to put their trust in him. Other young men of the time had visions of our country's future, and through the political meetings held in the towns they gained the support that was needed to bring about Confederation.

41. EARLY WESTERN SETTLEMENT

LET us imagine that we are pioneers, and that on a morning of early summer, in the year 1871, we have come to Fort Garry, now Winnipeg, in a Red River cart. We came from Eastern Canada to St. Paul in Minnesota by train, and from there we have travelled by boat and cart. In a few days we shall continue our journey westward, but before we do we must buy a cart, an ox, or perhaps a horse, harness, and supplies of food and other necessaries. An Indian on the street directs us to the Fort, and there we see a great pile of heavy harness. How can we find what we need? The piles are three or four feet deep. After an hour of rummaging we have reins, traces, and collar. We pay for these, and are then ready to go to an outfitter's for supplies. We buy sugar, salt, flour, and several large pieces of salted pork, and stow these in our cart, along with our blanket, small keg of nails, tools, and box of dishes and pans.

On the morning we are to continue our journey we take our place before dawn in a line of pioneers facing westward. The first cart in the line creaks up the rutty street, which is now Portage Avenue in Winnipeg, and soon we are out on the open plain. The sun grows hot, and we become tired, but there can be no pause yet in that steady, forward march. Not a moment of daylight can be wasted, but in the late dusky evening we make camp with the other travellers. Then we have a good meal of biscuits and fried pork, and if the mosquitoes leave us alone we soon fall asleep, wrapped in our blankets and lying on the ground. Next day, and for many days, we continue our journey in the same way.

After the first week the line of carts dwindles. Some of the pioneers have chosen homes along the way, but we, with others, press on towards Prince Albert. After a month, for the weather has been bright and the roads not too muddy, we are there, and with a sigh of relief we set out to choose our farm land and a site for our new home. We are sorry to bid farewell to our friends of

HOLY CROSS CHURCH, MACLEOD, ALBERTA, 1878.
(From a contemporary drawing by W. Armstrong.)
By kind permission of the John Ross Robertson Collection.

the road who are going on to Edmonton, but nevertheless we are glad to have no more days to spend in a creaking Red River cart.

.   .   .   .   .   .

In the year in which we made our imaginary journey, and for many years afterward, new settlers came to the West from Eastern Canada and from Europe.   German Mennonites founded a settlement in 1874 on the east side of the Red River, and two years later Icelanders settled on the shores of Lake Winnipeg.   By the year 1875 many little settlements were springing up in the West— Battleford, Lethbridge, Calgary, Edmonton, and others.   The town of our picture, Macleod, had so grown that in the year 1878, the year in which the picture was painted, it had a church and at least one house, which, probably, was a settlement store as well.

Many of the settlements of the West grew up near the North-West Mounted Police forts, but Lethbridge had a different origin. When the ranchers of Montana began to look for new cattle-grazing country they came up into what is now the province of Alberta, and there, on the banks of the Old Man River, a Montana trader saw a dark gleaming seam of rock that interested and excited him.   It was coal, and for a decade this trader " teamed " coal from the village of Lethbridge to Montana.

When the railway was being constructed in the West, little settlements sprang up as if overnight.   At first they were no more than store-houses and workers' boarding-houses.   Later, when settlers came and the railway itself furnished opportunities for shipping produce, these bare little villages grew into thriving, prosperous towns.

The opening of the West, first begun through the foresight of Lord Selkirk, is a tale of indomitable courage and achievement. Canadians can rightly be proud of the brave men and women who ventured across the trackless prairie, and who struggled year after year to break land and grow crops.

42. THE GUARDIANS OF THE PLAINS

WE have read about " The Company of Adventurers of England trading into Hudson's Bay," and of the charter King Charles II. gave them. In the year 1869, two hundred years after the first " Adventurers " had gone to Hudson Bay, the Company relinquished its right to the vast area of land stretching from Hudson Bay to Alaska.

This land then became part of the Dominion of Canada, and almost in a day hundreds of people began to prepare to go west to take up land. Many other hundreds would have prepared to go had they not been afraid of the Indians and of the lawlessness of a new country. Governor Archibald realized this, and in 1870 he asked Lieutenant William Butler to travel through the west and make recommendations of how settlers might be protected. In October 1870 Lieutenant Butler left Fort Garry on his long journey across nine hundred miles of prairie to the Rocky Mountains.

The Indians were worried because the buffalo was disappearing from the plains and because their land was being taken from them, and he learned of their fear and hatred of the white men. From the few settlers he heard many tales of dishonest traders who sold the Indians drugged whisky and stole their furs.

When Butler returned to Fort Garry he gave Governor Archibald a long report of his journey, and in it he recommended that a strong police force be sent to the plains. " The force must have no misfits or failures," Lieutenant Butler said, " and the men must not be stationed at fixed points or forts else they will afford little protection outside the immediate circle of these points." Another important recommendation which he made was that the force " should be independent of any faction or party."

Lieutenant Butler's report was well received by the Government officials, and in less than two years the first company of the Royal North-West Mounted Police was on its way to the prairie.

RED MEN AND WHITE MEN
(Cyro Cuneo, R.I.)
By kind permission of the Canadian Pacific Railway Co

But what a small unit it was, and how vast was their territory! Only one hundred and fifty men to patrol three hundred thousand square miles! No wonder that an urgent request was sent to Ottawa for reinforcements.

From the first the Mounted Police had the confidence of the Indians. They were fair in their dealings with them, and they were resolute and brave. In less than two years after they arrived on the prairie Chief Crowfoot of the warlike Blackfeet said, " They have protected us as the feather protects the bird from the frosts of winter." A splendid tribute surely, and, coming as it did from an old chief who had regarded the white man with bitter hatred, it is proof that the force was doing a great deal to reconcile the red men and the white.

One of the biggest tasks given to the men of the Force was that of making peace between the Indian tribes. The Blackfeet hated the Crees with an undying hatred, and almost at any time one tribe was ready to make war on the other. There is a splendid story of how Colonel Denny of the Force brought the leaders of the two tribes together to smoke the pipe of peace. A Cree Indian had been killed by a Blackfoot and the Crees were preparing to attack the Blackfoot encampment. Colonel Denny went to arrest the Blackfoot murderer, but when he found that he had disappeared he asked the Blackfoot chief to put up a peace lodge, " and I will bring the Cree chiefs," he promised.

When they came Colonel Denny explained to them that the Queen, their great mother, wished all her Indian children to live peacefully, and that she wanted them all to understand her laws. After the Indians had sat for a long time, and after they had smoked many pipes, the chiefs of the Crees shook hands with the chiefs of the Blackfeet, then the chiefs of the Blackfeet shook hands with the chiefs of the Crees, and finally, after they had all shaken hands with Colonel Denny, they departed, friends. And never afterward did the hatred of the one tribe for the other flame to battle heat.

There are many other stories of the courage and tact of the men of the Force, and if you would read tales of stirring adventure and of noble achievement you would do well to turn to the pages of their history.

43. THE BUILDING OF THE CANADIAN-PACIFIC RAILWAY

" I BELIEVE that many in this room will live to hear the whistle of the steam-engine in the passes of the Rocky Mountains and to make the journey from Halifax to the Pacific." These prophetic words were spoken by Joseph Howe in the year 1851, and they were the forerunners of many eager words and much effort to bind the far west of British North America to the distant east.

George Brown and Alexander Galt, long before the movement for Confederation was looked on with favour, had worked diligently in the cause of railway building in the west. They felt that a railway would be a strong influence for national unity, and in 1871, when British Columbia became a province of the Dominion of Canada, the citizens of the far west made one important demand; it was that an overland railway be built to the coast within ten years. Although the undertaking seemed impossible to many Canadians, especially as several engineers and surveyors had reported that no suitable pass could be found through the mountains, Sir John A. Macdonald promised that the railroad would be built.

The difficulties were even greater than were anticipated. Although the company was at first able to raise large sums of money, the work was no more than half done when the funds were depleted. They could not borrow from the public or from the banks, and were forced to appeal to the Government for help. With many misgivings, Sir John A. Macdonald's government agreed to advance the necessary money, and at last the bands of steel were completed.

" Stand fast, Craigellachie ! " As Donald Smith shouted the old Highland battle-cry, he drove the last spike of the railroad into its place. As the ring of his hammer was echoed from the mountain peaks a great shout rose from the throng of people. It was a shout of joy and thanksgiving, for the task that had occupied

BUILDING OF THE CANADIAN-PACIFIC RAILWAY, 1886.
(*E. J. Dinsmore.*)

Canadian statesmen and financiers, and more than three thousand workers, for over twenty years was now completed. At last bands of steel linked Eastern Canada with the Dominion's far western province of British Columbia.

It had been a gigantic undertaking. It had needed sincere faith in Canada's future, and it had called for hard and constant work that seemed never-ending, for the rails had to be laid through forests, over swamps and rivers, over prairies, through rocks and mountains. Great gangs of surveyors, timber-cutters, graders, bridge-builders, and track-layers had worked for years, and now, on this November day in 1885, three thousand miles of railway tracks stretched across Canada, bringing the east to the west and the west to the east.

As the people were standing before the mountain pass through which, in a few months, the first train from Montreal to Vancouver would thunder, a message was flashed across the Atlantic. It was from Queen Victoria, and it read: "Congratulations on the completion of the Canadian-Pacific Railway. It is of great importance to the whole British Empire."

It is a far cry from that memorable November day, but could those who toiled and struggled to build the Canadian-Pacific see to what lengths their early endeavours have extended, great indeed would be their satisfaction and pride.

44. HYDRO-ELECTRIC POWER

PIONEER towns and villages in Upper Canada nearly always grew up about mills or mill sites. Mills were built near the rapids of swift-flowing streams, so that the mill-wheels could be turned by the flow of water. By itself, however, the water was not strong enough to create much power, and dams were built to hold it back. When a sluice or gate was opened the water rushed through with a roar, and turned the mill-wheel more rapidly than the stream alone could do. By this means the grain of pioneer Canadians was ground into flour and the logs sawn into lumber. Even when the steam-engine was perfected most water-power mills were kept in use, for they cost little to run.

After the invention of the steam-engine, the next important step was the discovery of how to use electricity, and how to produce electric current with a dynamo. As soon as engineers had learned to harness the steam-engine to the dynamo, electricity became a practical form of power, and in this way, as early as the year 1880, streets and houses began to be lit by it. This means of lighting was very expensive in Ontario because of the lack of coal, and engineers soon found a way to use water-power instead of steam as the motive force for generating electricity. At first the electric current could be carried only for a short distance, but by increasing the pressure or voltage the radius of distribution was gradually made wider. A few years later the British engineer, Ferranti, succeeded in carrying electricity a distance of ten miles.

Now the greatest water-power in America is Niagara Falls, and a few years after Ferranti's achievement, and after American engineers were already carrying electrical power a distance of forty-one miles, Canadians and Americans began considering the electrical possibilities of Niagara Falls. By the year 1900 electricity was being generated at the Falls, and being carried to various border towns and cities of the United States.

The Americans were benefiting so greatly from the hydro-electric power of Niagara that people in Ontario were eager to

SIR ADAM BECK TURNING ON THE HYDRO-ELECTRIC CURRENT AT BADEN,
ONTARIO
(*Fergus Kyle.*)

find out how they could use it. In 1902 representatives of various municipalities of western Ontario met in Berlin, Ontario, to discuss its possibilities, and to decide how the power should be distributed. One of the representatives was Adam Beck, then the Mayor of London, Ontario, and a year later, when the Government appointed a commission to investigate the matter, Mr. (later Sir Adam) Beck was asked to be a member.

He at once began to make a thorough study of the subject, and in less than two years electrical power was being sent to many towns in western Ontario ; it lighted homes and factories ; it ran engines and street cars. A few years later the power of Niagara was being distributed throughout western Ontario, and hydro-electric plants were established in other parts of Canada, and to-day every city of the Dominion is supplied with hydro-electric power for lighting, for running machinery in factories, and for household appliances. Thousands of small towns and villages and remote sawmills throughout the country have hydro-electric power, and hundreds of farms are equipped with electrically run implements.

Our illustration shows Sir Adam Beck turning on the hydro-electric power to illuminate the dark streets of his native village of Baden. It was on a cold night in December 1911 ; during the day throngs of people gathered in Baden from the countryside and the villages near by in order to see the streets suddenly filled with this new and wonderful light. We are so accustomed to electricity that we can hardly imagine what it meant to people whose only artificial light was that of candles or of coal-oil lamps. While the streets were still dark, the village band played lively tunes by torchlight. The crowd was greatest in front of the little opera house, where all eyes were turned to the balcony. Dim figures appeared through the windows and moved towards the white board on which an electrical switch had been installed. Without warning, the darkness was broken by the blinding light of the arc-lamps, and the last notes of the band were drowned in the cheers of the people as they recognized Sir Adam Beck with his hand on the switch.

It was a great day for Baden, and in a few years electricity was in common use throughout Canada.

45. CANADA'S PART IN WORLD WAR ONE

EARLY in August 1914 the war clouds that had for years been hanging over Europe burst into flames that destroyed millions of people and caused untold misery, which is being suffered even to this day.

Germany, Austria, and Turkey were fighting Russia on their north side, and France and Serbia on their south. Britain was not directly concerned in the quarrel, but when Germany invaded the neutral territory of Belgium she had no choice but to throw in her lot with France. At Ottawa the Houses of Parliament at once decided that Canada would fight shoulder to shoulder with Britain and France.

Within a few weeks over thirty thousand Canadians had embarked for service overseas. It required many large steamships to carry so many men, and this was the largest collection of ships ever seen on the St. Lawrence since Admiral Saunders carried Wolfe and his regiments safely up the river. The troop-ships assembled in Gaspé Basin, where Cartier had landed nearly four hundred years before. Here the ships were met by cruisers of the British navy and escorted safely across the Atlantic to England. The winter was spent in rigorous training in camp on Salisbury Plain, and in the spring the First Canadian Division took its place in the trenches.

In the long line of men and guns and mud that stretched from the North Sea across Belgium and France to the Swiss frontier, the Canadians held only a narrow frontage, measuring about three miles. But that section, though small, was of tremendous importance, since it covered the town of Ypres, through which lay the road to the English Channel. If the Germans could break through at Ypres, and capture Calais or Boulogne, they would cut off the British army from its base of supplies.

One dull afternoon in April 1915 great yellow clouds were seen coming from the German trenches and drifting with the

CANADIANS AT YPRES

wind towards the Canadian line. It was a poison gas, and all who breathed it were seized with an agonizing fit of choking and coughing. The Germans had added this new horror to warfare, and its unexpected terror might well have stampeded the bravest troops. The Canadians, however, not only stood firm, but even extended their line to close the gap left by the retreat of other troops. For seven days and nights they fought against tremendous odds and prevented the German armies from breaking through. " Their gallantry and determination," said the official report, " undoubtedly saved the day."

Three other Canadian divisions were organized, and the Canadian Corps won a great name for itself. Their capture of Vimy Ridge showed intelligence, discipline, and skill, as well as bravery.

The part Canada played in World War One was important to the Allied cause, but it was even more important to Canada itself. It made Canadians realize that they were now a nation, with responsibilities of its own. A mighty united effort and the noble sacrifice of fifty thousand dead had deepened from coast to coast the sense of a common heritage. When the Peace Treaty was concluded, the signature of Sir Robert L. Borden, Prime Minister of Canada, appeared among those of the other combatants. It meant that Canada was now recognized by the great Powers as a nation in her own right.

46. THE BUILDING OF ROADS

RAILWAY building made great progress in Canada during the nineteenth century. The old post-chaise and its four prancing horses were replaced by railway carriages and steam-engines. The postman who had ridden along trails and corduroy roads had no longer need of saddle-bags and horses, for mail was sent by train, and the postman himself became a mail clerk or a postmaster.

Although the railways offered many opportunities for travel and for the shipment of farm produce, lumber, and minerals, and made possible the opening up of distant parts of the land, the " fever " of railway building did have at least one bad effect. The roads of the country were neglected. Property owners were required to do " road work " every year, but the roads continued to be deep in mud during the spring and autumn, and rutty and dusty in the summer. Although towns sprang up along the railway lines farmers still found it difficult to get their produce to market and their grain to the mill.

The first efforts to improve the roads of the country were made when private companies leased certain main highways, kept them in repair with gravel and macadam, and charged a toll to those who passed over them. The people soon became dissatisfied with these " toll " roads, however, and began to demand " roads of their own." Consequently certain counties made out road-building programmes, and, aided by grants from the province, were able to build good gravel roads.

In 1907, however, and indeed before that year, the need for other than ordinary " horse " roads appeared. With the arrival of the automobile and its sudden growth in popularity, road experts realized that a change must be made in road building and repair. The condition of Canadian roads at that time is well described in an automobile advertisement, " It has power, good lines, is luxurious in finish and appointments, but best of all it can stand the rack and wear of Canadian roads."

By the year 1912 automobiles in Ontario alone numbered over

[PLATE 46.

BUILDING THE MOTOR ROADS
(Fergus Kyle.)

twelve thousand, and several years later all the provinces of the Dominion began building motor roads. Automobiles were licensed, and the money obtained from licence fees was devoted to road building. Long highways, very different from the old " horse " roads, were built. These new roads were made of concrete, asphalt, or tarred macadam. Steep, dangerous hills were cut down, and bridges and viaducts were built. Between the years of 1914 and 1930 over thirty thousand miles of road were paved or rebuilt in the province of Ontario alone, and to-day in the whole Dominion there are more than four hundred thousand miles of highways.

Farmers to-day no longer have difficulty in taking their produce to market. Indeed they are now able to market much of their produce at their own gates, for the automobile not only brings farm people to town, but it takes many town dwellers to the country. The highway has become one of the chief factors not only of trade but of pleasure.

Our illustration shows the work of road-building in progress. It is interesting to compare the number of workers engaged in road building in 1930 with the number engaged in building the Canadian Pacific Railway in 1885. There were many more work-men in 1885, and many more machines, implements, and tools in 1930.

That was in 1930. The number of highways extended and the mileage of good roads now actually completed, or nearly so, pales the 1930 figures into relative insignificance.

47. THE AEROPLANE IN CANADA

EVERYONE knows the story of the Athenian Daedalus: that he made wings for himself and his son, Icarus, and they flew away from Minos; but only Daedalus reached Italy, for Icarus flew so close to the sun that the sun's heat melted the wax on his wings and he fell into the sea. This ancient story typifies the experiments of would-be fliers: something gained, something lost, and the losses so disastrous that for several centuries only very audacious men—or those considered foolhardy—attempted to fly.

However, about the turn of our century, it became evident that an era was looming which would be marked by intense and persistent experiments in aviation, and that many of these efforts would be conducted in North America, as this continent stood to benefit greatly from the development of aviation providing, of course, that the aeroplane could be used extensively in industry and commerce. Prophets of aviation foresaw the 'plane, then called the flying machine, assisting Canada in the growth she most desired—that of settlement. Suppose immigrants could be flown to their new homes. . . . Suppose supplies, foodstuffs, tools, implements, could be dropped from the sky. . . . Those with prospective vision saw pioneering losing its hazards.

In 1903 the United States Government allotted fifty thousand dollars for research in aviation, and at the end of the year, at Kitty Hawk in North Carolina, the first flight in which a person was carried from the ground by mechanical means only was accomplished. A little more than five years later, on February 23, 1909, Dr. Alexander Graham Bell, the renowned inventor of the telephone, stood on the ice of Baddeck Bay in Nova Scotia, watching his associate, J. D. McCurdy, fly their 'plane, the *Silver Dart*, for the first time. The 'plane rose slowly and steadily to thirty feet and in three-quarters of a minute flew half a mile. So, almost obscurely, for not much notice was taken of the *Silver Dart's* airworthiness, Canadian aviation began.

Now came a long period of trial and error to get the flying

[PLATE 47.

AEROPLANE AND FOREST FIRE
(*Fergus Kyle.*)

machine to a state where it could make long sustained flights. There is no record of how many experiments were made, but Canada, like every other country, had her failures and near successes. In 1911 an American, Rodgers, completed the first transcontinental flight, but people were more amused than impressed, for he had been forty-nine days in going from one coast to the other.

Three more years of trial and error and improvement! No one will ever know how much feverish experimenting was done on the beaches of Canada's inland lakes and in sequestered, shallow, broad valleys. It was plain that air transport was to be achieved to the accompaniment of great rivalry and the piling up of records. Scientists regretted this; daring young men were thrilled. In 1914 war broke out; now was aviation's chance to prove its worth. Four squadrons of twelve aeroplanes were attached to the first contingent of the British expeditionary army, but no one knew exactly how they would be used. For reconnaissance, the military command decided, but soon confident young men, a score or more of Canadians among them, were saying that, armed with rifles and hand grenades, the pilots could conduct offensive and defensive war. By 1915 air-training stations were set up in Canada and soon Canadian-crewed 'planes were sharing in the thick of battle —scouting, fighting, and dropping bombs on the enemy's territory. When the war ended in 1919, even the most doubting Thomas believed the air age was well begun.

In most countries the first commercial work assigned to fliers was mail service, but in Canada the first commercial ventures for the pilots recently returned from World War One and eager to roam the sky, focused around the development of our natural resources and the allied necessary protection of the frontiers of sparsely settled territory. Financed by enterprising men like James A. Richardson of Winnipeg, this air service expanded in the northern parts of our Dominion, even inaugurating an air-mail service, and lead eventually to the establishment of the vast regular air transport lines which flit to and fro, not only to all parts of Canada but to far-distant lands as well.

In 1928 the aeroplane was used to assist in the building of the Hudson Bay Railroad, both for transporting supplies and for general survey duty. The Dominion Government engaged airmen to patrol the Straits daily during the summer, taking numerous photographs, observing the direction and timing the speed of drifting ice, and keeping systematic records of the weather. With the knowledge thus secured the engineers were able to build road-beds strong enough to withstand varying pressures of ice. A similar and much better-equipped service assisted in the building of the Alcan Highway during World War Two. When the war ended, the weather stations of Canada were placed under the supervision of the Royal Canadian Air Force.

Although the Dominion Government did not begin regular mail service across the country as soon as the United States, many private companies carried mail and supplies to distant outposts. When the Peace River country was being opened up in the late 'twenties and early 'thirties, settlers and their effects were transported by 'plane. On one occasion a 'plane transported a yoke of oxen. Edmonton, at this time, became one of the most important taking-off places, not only for immigrants but for mining engineers, and geologists searching for oil. When very hardy wheat, the result of much experimenting, was grown in the " Peace," it was flown out for sale and distribution for seed. Even before World War Two great 'plane loads of grain were transported to storage elevators in the more accessible parts of the country.

In April 1937, by act of Parliament, a national transportation scheme was instituted and given the name of Trans-Canada Air Lines. A few months later, on 1st September, the first flight of the system was accomplished—from Vancouver to Seattle. Very soon after this Trans-Canada began a regular daily service from coast to coast. To-day not only Trans-Canada but private companies as well span the vast distances of Canada regularly and maintain flight services with many places in the United States, and with Great Britain and distant parts of the far-flung British Empire. 'Plane journeys to any part of the world can be arranged as easily as rail and ship passage.

The Canadian Pacific Air Lines serve in a special way vast and thinly settled areas of northern and western Canada. Their traffic is more limited in revenue, in miles flown, and passengers carried, but their services are vital to many a frontier of settlement and industry. By the Canadian Pacific Air Lines you can reach the centres of the pulp and paper, and aluminum manufacture in the Saguenay region of Quebec ; and along the Pacific Coast the Canadian Pacific Air Lines render service of inestimable value.

In the far North-West the Canadian Pacific aircraft will take you to Whitehorse in the Yukon, to Dawson, and even to Aklavik on the Arctic Ocean. From your luxurious airliner you descend into a strange, primitive world of Eskimos and Arctic solitudes. C.P.A.L., as it is commonly called, or one of the many smaller private planes, carry those who must travel to or from otherwise inaccessible northern outposts. By their routes, also, tourists and holiday-seekers can visit many far-northern resorts of continent-wide fame.

When World War Two ended, the Royal Canadian Air Force set up search and rescue squadrons with control stations at strategic points across the Dominion. The men of this service go out on the most dangerous peace-time expeditions imaginable. In 1949, for instance, a rescue mission of 5,570 miles was accomplished in $44\frac{1}{2}$ hours, a record at that time. This was from Greenwood, Nova Scotia, to Resolute Bay, nine hundred miles south of the North Pole, and thence to Montreal. " Search and Rescue " has at its command the best and most up-to-date equipment, and every station has men trained to be para-rescuers. We are constantly reading of the wonders accomplished by the skilled and daring pilots and crews of this renowned service.

The aeroplane is constantly changing and being improved. The one shown in Plate 47 was quite a marvel in its day. You will be interested in comparing it with the 'planes of to-day.

48. INDUSTRIAL DEVELOPMENT IN CANADA

DURING the twentieth century far-reaching developments have taken place in Canadian industry. Consider our vast extent of half a continent and our abundant resources of forest, mines, fisheries, and farm lands which provide raw materials for manufacturing. Romantic and startling are the stories one could tell of each of these resources, but space limits us to but a passing reference.

What would you say is Canada's leading manufacturing industry?

One cannot predict the future, but the making of pulp and paper from our vast forests of coniferous trees and other softwoods will likely always be one of our leading single manufactures in peace-time. It is a diversified process. The logs are felled in fragrant wind-swept forests. At the pulp and paper mills processes are continued for the production of fine quality papers, newsprint, tar-paper, cardboard, fibre wallboard, and other pulp products. Large quantities of our pulp and newsprint are exported, chiefly to the United States.

Agriculture in all its branches remains our basic primary industry. Changing times, however, have developed and transformed it in a way that would surprise the farmer of Confederation days. Combines, tractors, trucks, milking machines, threshing machines, and other equipment now perform rapidly the work of many men and women and draught animals. Thus the manufacture of farm machinery has become an important industry.

Wheat and flour are leading Canadian exports as our prairie provinces form one of the great bread-baskets of the world. Construction of grain elevators has been a great building project, while storing and transporting the crop by lake and ocean vessels, and to a lesser extent by air, is a vast annual undertaking. The raising of livestock, meat packing, the dairy industry producing milk, butter, cheese, condensed and powdered milk, combine agriculture and manufacturing. The growing of cereal grains, cultivation of vegetables and fruits, production of honey and beet sugar add to the volume and value of our farm products. From all these agricultural activities our own people are fed and many, many million dollars' worth of exports are sent abroad.

As the country and the population grew, farming expanded in various minor directions also. Tobacco raising, for instance, has become of increasing importance in the Lake Erie district of Ontario. Throughout the Dominion fur farming supplements the supply of pelts obtained by trapping wild animals. By means of this twofold source Canada maintains her centuries-old position as one of the foremost fur-producing countries of the world.

In regard to our mining industry and mineral deposits, some of the facts and figures are really breath-taking. The mysterious geological ages of the past were kind to Canada. The great Canadian Shield or Laurentian Highland, which encircles Hudson Bay and comprises about half of Canada's total area, is a rich storehouse of metallic wealth. The Rocky Mountain region of western Canada and the Appalachian area of eastern Canada are also important for their mineral deposits.

Canadian mines are world famous for production of gold and nickel. Over fifty per cent. of the world's asbestos is mined in the eastern townships of Quebec. Our Dominion produces almost a quarter of the cobalt of the world, as well as large quantities of copper, silver, lead, iron, zinc, and the very precious ore from which radium is obtained.

In the estimated coal reserves of the world Canada is surpassed only by the United States. This indicates valuable coal mining when future settlement and development will make the industry profitable. Resources of petroleum and natural gas, found in limited quantities in Ontario, were known for long years to be hidden away in the vast Canadian West. However, " oil " remained comparatively quiescent until the Turner Valley developments brought the West into prominence as a potential large-scale source. But 1947 was the banner year for the western oilfields when Alberta's Leduc operations definitely established the area as a vast oil reservoir, the magnitude of which is fantastic.

Fishing is Canada's oldest industry. It is a pursuit fraught with the hardihood of the sailor and the romance of the sea, with tales of storm and conflict, of heroic survival or tragic bereavement.

Both salt- and fresh-water fishing provide many species for commercial purposes and for testing the sportsman's skill. Fish processing is carried on at the canneries for salmon, lobster, sardines, and so forth, and also at freezing and drying plants.

Transportation and communication have become completely revolutionized within the last century, and Canada has kept pace with all these marvels of modern times. Construction and repair of railway tracks, building of railway rolling-stock, telegraph- and telephone-line equipment, radio stations and sets are responsible for many growing industries. Production of automobiles, aircraft, vessels, and boats for lake and ocean traffic requires the employment of many thousands of men and women.

As one would expect, industrial progress has been accompanied by a shifting of population from rural to urban districts. By a recent census, urban population exceeded rural by about one million, and the growth of manufacturing and of urban centres is steadily increasing. Some of Canada's newest and largest industrial plants are concerned with the manufacturing of aluminum, nylon, rayon, and synthetic rubber.

In volume of external trade, Canada ranks high in international circles. Our weakness is that with a small population our domestic market is limited and we are particularly dependent upon foreign markets. It is, therefore, especially important that Canadians maintain a well-informed and wise foreign policy.

49. THE YEARS BETWEEN

THE chapter on Canada's part in World War One ends with, "Canada was now recognized by the great Powers as a nation in her own right," and although this was true our country still had to pass through a severe testing period. Even before Sir Robert Borden, then Prime Minister, signed the treaty of peace at Versailles, unrest began to bubble and seethe throughout the country.

Factories that had been engaged in making war supplies had to close down. This meant unemployment; and coupled with it was a great rise in the cost of living. Eggs sold as high as ninety cents a dozen, and bacon soared to a dollar a pound, with other foodstuffs following their lead. Rents leaped to double what they had been before the war, and farmers, lumbermen, and miners realized that the market for their essential commodities must shrink. Nation-wide uneasiness reached a peak in Winnipeg in the spring of 1919 when a general strike was called in that city and did not collapse until the Government sent troops.

The Winnipeg strike let the Government know that it must not dally over a programme of re-establishment. Within the next two years more than half a million dollars was spent in war service gratuities, in loans to soldiers who wanted to purchase land, and in training returned men for peace-time vocations.

It was fortunate that Canada was well started on peace-time activities, for soon another enemy confronted her. This was world-wide depression which first attacked agriculture, causing the price of wheat to tumble to a near all-time low. The next industry to suffer was mining, and miners from all over the country flocked to cities looking for work in factories.

The depression became so serious that many nations, Canada being one, sent representatives to an international economic conference in Genoa, and partly as a result of tariff agreements reached there the depression abated. For a few years the economic outlook appeared very rosy; the stock markets in Toronto and Montreal boomed. Everyone, it seemed, except farmers (for the price of agricultural products remained low) had great wealth almost in the palm of his hand. Then the enormous balloon of trading collapsed. The break came first in New York's Wall Street, but the repercussions soon reached Canada. Mr. Mackenzie King's Government that had achieved political status of nationhood for Canada at an Imperial Conference in London was swept out of office, and the Conservative Party took over the affairs of the nation.

Never before had Canadians looked so anxiously to their Government for assistance. The new Prime Minister, R. B. Bennett, would have needed a magic wand to aid him in accomplishing all the things the citizens wanted, and when the speech from the throne was read in March 1931, it seemed to many that Mr. Bennett had such a wand firmly grasped in his two hands. There were to be old age pensions, help for farmers, extensive highways, many reforms in tariff, educational grants paid to the provinces, and an Imperial Conference was to plan how the various parts of the British Empire could work together to master the ogre of depression. There was something else remarkable about this speech from the throne : it was the first throne speech to be broadcast. Canadians everywhere in the Dominion could hear it ; since that time all throne speeches have been broadcast.

The Conservative Government set to work with a will to carry out its programme. The Imperial Conference met ; the Prime Minister went to Washington to confer with the American Government on tariff regulations ; old age pensions were instituted ; grants were voted to farmers. Despite the apparent diligence of the Government, however, the people generally were dissatisfied, and at the next election the Liberals, led as formerly by Mackenzie King, returned to office.

Depression continued ; in western Canada its severity was intensified by drought and dust storms. Vast tracts that had produced the finest wheat ever grown were now barren or were dotted with thistles. Worse, war was darkening the horizon of the world.

Less than a decade before, Canada's delegate to the League of Nations at Geneva had acted as president of the Assembly, and in 1928 Canada's Prime Minister, Mackenzie King, had been called to the League's Council. Perhaps because our statesmen had taken so active a part in the League's work, Canadians generally had come to believe that the League could avert war, and now there was much opposition to the Government embarking on an expensive programme for defence. Nevertheless, air-training was intensified, and air-fields at Trenton, Camp Borden, and Calgary were extended to accommodate the growing number of cadets. The Royal Canadian Navy, which comprised less than a thousand men for destroyers and three minesweepers, was also extended, and fishermen on the west and east coasts were instructed in naval warfare. As unostentatiously as possible the militia, organized in eleven districts, was being strengthened by training not only in the districts but in the Officers' Training Corps of the universities and at the Royal Military College at Kingston.

Those Canadians who pinned their faith on the League of Nations could not believe that war must be the inevitable outcome of the growth of Fascism in Italy, the amazingly rapid spread of Nazism in Germany, and the steady advancement of militarism in Japan. Many others considered that our distance from the scenes of invasion and unrest precluded North America from war. True, Japan had taken Manchuria from China and was making war in China's coastal waters ; true, Mussolini of Italy had taken Albania ; and true, Adolf Hitler of Germany had marched into Austria and Czechoslovakia, and was demanding the return to Germany of Danzig, which had been made a free city after World War One. True, true, true, but were the ideologies that inspired and justified these acts of aggression a menace to our democratic way of life ? All through the summer of 1939, with anxiety increasing daily, people all over North America asked this question and answered it fearfully and dubiously. In the early morning of 1st September the question was definitely and irrevocably answered.

50. AGAIN WAR

THE answer which came on September 1, 1939, was in the world's most brutal language—the firing of guns. These were fired from a German battleship, and the target was a Polish garrison stationed on the Danzig Peninsula for the purpose of guarding munition stores and dumps. Adolf Hitler stated that he had " counter-attacked." No initial attack had preceded his counter !

At the same time as the German ship was firing her guns, German soldiers were approaching the Polish border, heading for Warsaw, the capital city of Poland. At once Britain and France, who had promised to aid Poland if she were attacked, issued an ultimatum which said that if Nazi troops were not withdrawn they would go to Poland's assistance. Germany ignored the ultimatum, and when she ignored a second, issued on 3rd September, Great Britain and France declared a state of war.

Great Britain's declaration did not involve the Dominions, for their new status within the Empire gave them the right to decide whether they would or would not go to war. In Canada, as in Australia, New Zealand, South Africa, and Eire, participation or neutrality became the one problem of national importance and of individual importance as well. No one but felt that the course of his life hung in the balance of war or neutrality.

The Prime Minister summoned Parliament. Probably no member had ever before so poignantly felt the grave responsibility of his mandate to represent people in the House of Commons. The debate began on Thursday, 7th September, and Canadians kept close to their radios, fearing, hoping, and intermittently believing they knew what the result would be. On 10th September the decision was made and King George broadcast Canada's proclamation of war. All the British Dominions, except Eire, voted to participate in the conflict.

Before September ended, the conquest of Poland was complete ; Germany had the west, and Russia, who had entered the eastern part in the middle of the month, had the east. The first bloody

Blitzkrieg was over, a victory for the enemy. Germany and the opposing forces aligned themselves along the Rhine, the French and British in the Maginot Line, the Germans behind their West Wall.

In the meantime Canada was preparing for active service. Two days after she declared war, the largest budget ever presented to Parliament was approved, and this, perhaps more than the call for men to join the services, impressed citizens generally with how serious a view our statesmen and military leaders took of the war. It would not be brief; on all sides one heard whispers of " six years." Four years had been needed for victory in World War One, and this would take half as long again ! Soon after the budget was passed, the Government set to work doing sound economic planning so that there would be no inflation and no unfair distribution of foodstuffs. Ceilings were soon put on rents and most essential commodities. In World War One Canada's effort had not been confined to the combat services, nor would it be in this war. Food would be needed for the armies of Great Britain and France and for the civilian populations. Again Canada was to be a " bread-basket," and the basket was to be well stocked with meat, fish, flour, butter, eggs, cheese, and vegetables.

Through the autumn of 1939 and the winter of 1940 the armies in Europe kept steadfast watch across the Rhine, but there was little fighting. People began to murmur, " Phoney war," but the military leaders were not lulled into idleness. In England and Scotland training fields and barracks were being prepared for troops of the Dominions who, after receiving primary instruction in their native lands, would be given their battle training close to the likely combat areas.

In Canada men of the Dominions, Great Britain, and Northern Ireland were working out the largest military co-operation scheme ever undertaken up to that time : it was for the training in Canada of airmen from Canada, the United Kingdom, Australia, and New Zealand. Nine air-fields were to be used and the scheme, inaugurated on December 17, 1939, was called the British Commonwealth Air Training Plan. Norwegian, Dutch, and Danish airmen who escaped from their native lands after the Germans invaded them in 1940 were trained in Canada also. From this B.C.A.T.P. over

85,000 men emerged to fly Allied 'planes and fight the enemy, and of this output over fifty per cent. were Canadian. Little wonder that Canada was often referred to as the great aerodrome of the allied countries.

The winter of 1940 and the " phoney war " ended simultaneously. When Norway and the Low Countries were invaded, people knew that the war was truly serious.

At this time Canadians began asking about the Royal Canadian Navy, but their questions could not be answered—not because the navy was neglecting its duty but because the answers were " top drawer " secrets. They concerned not only our safety but that of a life-line of soldiers and food being transported under convoy across the Atlantic. They concerned also the designing and testing and successful operation of a new snub-nosed, swift little boat called the corvette that was used for hunting submarines. And besides, minesweepers manned by Canadians, many of whom a short while before had been Yarmouth, Digby, and Bridgewater fishermen, were being launched at a rate that had been considered impossible before the war. By 1945 three hundred and sixty-eight Canadian ships were in operation in the seaways of the world.

The first Canadian soldiers to leave Canada for combat service went to Newfoundland and Labrador to assist in guarding those important frontiers. Before the summer of 1940 arrived, Canadian soldiers were in Britain being further trained to man tanks and to be paratroopers, and, above all else, to be steady, dependable alert infantrymen skilled in the essential day-to-day duties of hard warfare. There would be no great adventures and nothing glamorous, so it was said, in the life of the soldier in this war. But the prophets were wrong ; the first Canadian soldiers to arrive in Britain were called on to assist in one of the boldest and most hazardous undertakings of the war.

The Netherlands and Luxembourg were soon overwhelmed by Germany's crack soldiers who invaded on 10th March, but in Belgium furious resistance was put up by the Belgians, French, and British. Liége, Louvain, Namur, all cities that had tried to withstand the Germans in World War One, again fell, and before the month ended it was evident that Belgium must succumb. On 28th May the King of the Belgians gave his army orders to cease fire. The British and French fought on desperately, their backs to the sea. All the way to Dunkirk and on the sands they fought, and there the weary men who had begun to school themselves for death or imprisonment saw a most wonderful thing : the sea beyond the broad beaches was full of little boats and men. Britishers of almost every trade and profession comprised the rescuers, and with them were Canadian soldiers getting their first taste of war. In a few days nearly four hundred thousand French and British soldiers were taken from Dunkirk and across the channel to safety in England. Then France collapsed. Great Britain and the Dominions were alone in the struggle against Nazi Germany.

Soon after, the Battle of Britain began and the first squadrons of the Royal Canadian Air Force to leave Canada took an active part in beating back the furious attacks. Day after day, and night after night, the *Luftwaffe* bombarded Britain's arsenals, naval bases, and industrial plants. The Canadians who helped in the defence of Britain were those who had been trained before the war. Their first experience of being subjected to enemy fire was surpassed in fury only by the attacks made nearly two years later when the allied air forces carried on constant and daring bombardment of enemy strongholds, coastal fortifications, the industrial Ruhr Valley, and Cologne.

Early in the war when newspapers began printing stories about Commandos, few people had any idea what Commandos were. In August 1942 Canadians had the meaning of Commandos indelibly impressed upon them, for ten thousand Canadian soldiers —Commandos—raided the French coastal town of Dieppe where, it was believed, the Germans were preparing for an invasion of Great Britain. The Canadians were screened by Canadian, American, and British 'planes, and in their penetration of the town they were assisted by French soldiers who had been based in England since Dunkirk. A great deal of damage was inflicted on the German fortifications, but many of the Commandos were killed, seriously injured, or taken prisoner.

Seven months before, a disaster of great magnitude had befallen Canada. Soldiers who had been sent to participate in the defence of Hong Kong were forced to surrender to the Japanese. This happened on Christmas Day 1941, and probably will be known for many decades as Canada's black Christmas. Seven weeks after this surrender a second one took place in the East, that of Singapore.

In December of 1941, after Japan attacked Pearl Harbour, one of the American bastions of the Pacific, the United States allied herself as a fighting force against the Axis powers.

Although 1941 and 1942 were crowded with discouragement the tide of battle was steadily turning and Canadians approached 1943 very hopefully. The campaign in Italy was going well ; three hundred thousand Fascists had surrendered to the British and Canadians in Greece. When it became known that the first Canadian infantry division was in Sicily (1943), people at home, having been informed of the achievements of the joint air forces in northern Italy, thought they could see the course to be taken : first, pincers on Italy ; next, a frontal attack on the north-west French coast, and next—soon—capitulation of the enemy. This is what happened, but not in 1943. D-Day came in the early summer of 1944, and after it nearly a year of steady fighting and marching. Canadians, after having nibbled for a long time on the toe and heel of Italy's boot, made a slow and tedious march northward. Other Canadians, jointly with the British, Americans, and Free French, began a long, onerous trek towards Germany, fighting most of the way. Before Christmas 1944 most of Holland was free. Final victory in Europe was a matter of time ; months, weeks, days. It came in May 1945, and in August Japan capitulated. Less only a few days, we had had a six-year war.

This is a very brief account which tells nothing of the bravery and faithfulness of the Canadian Women's Auxiliary forces, nor of the thousands of men and women who were employed in the war plants set up throughout the country. Thousands of 'planes, motor vehicles, cargo and patrol ships, and vast supplies of guns and ammunition were produced in Canada. Much of this material, along with huge quantities of food and clothing, was sent to the various allied nations.

51. NEWFOUNDLAND, CANADA'S TENTH PROVINCE

" BRITAIN's oldest colony " has been the time-honoured claim of the people of Newfoundland. Many ties of sentiment, race, religion, and climatic and island-bred similarity linked this island of the North Atlantic to its mother country of Great Britain. Geographically a part of the North American continent, it is in spirit and tradition an outpost of the United Kingdom.

Newfoundland has had a varied political experience ranging through the stages of Responsible Government (acquired in 1855), Dominion status, then Commission of Government inaugurated in 1934 to meet the financial crisis caused by the stagnation of world trade. In 1949 the island (42,734 square miles in area) and its dependency of Labrador (110,000 square miles) added to our Dominion a territory nearly one and two-thirds the size of the United Kingdom. The population, however, was, by the 1945 census, only about 325,000.

Throughout the centuries fishing has been the main industry of this island people. Cod, herring, seal, lobster, and whale constitute the sea harvest. Dried cod and cod-liver oil rank very high in value, but after the outbreak of World War Two, when orders for fish literally poured in, a very active fresh frozen-fish enterprise developed. In earlier days the majority of the people lived on the coast, and men won their livelihood from arduous, adventurous struggle in their small craft and sailing vessels. Little wonder that Newfoundlanders have a personality of their own fostered by such rugged living and by contact with the hills and the sea !

In more recent years lumbering and forest industries, mining, development of hydro-electric power, and promotion of agriculture have given more regular and diversified employment. At Corner Brook and at Grand Falls vast pulp and paper mills have been established. The development at Corner Brook, on the west coast at the mouth of the Humber River, is of great importance. In addition to the full-time employees it gives work to thousands of men at logging in winter—a very valuable complement of the spring-to-autumn fishing season. Corner Brook has developed a splendid harbour, steamers, plant, and a fine modern town.

Valuable iron ore is mined at Bell Island in Conception Bay near St. John's. Large high-grade iron ore deposits exist in Labrador also. Other minerals include coal, zinc, lead, copper ; and in Labrador the hunt for gold which is known to exist is expanding.

Quaint names enrich the geography of Newfoundland. Where else would one expect to find Goose and Gander airports ! Gander Airport, in north-western Newfoundland, is one of the greatest crossways of the world. Trans-Canada Air Lines, British Airways, and several foreign lines, including those of the United States, the Netherlands, and Sweden, use the facilities of this vast trans-Atlantic base. Goose Airport, in Labrador, is an alternative landing field farther north. It will play an ever-expanding part as a strategic and commercial base, as well as a pivotal point for mercy flights, and for scientific and geological expeditions.

In the middle years of the nineteenth century Newfoundland was a landing place and great link in uniting Great Britain and America by cable. In the middle of this present century the military and strategic importance of this province has become outstanding. Under an agreement with the British Government in 1942, the United States leased three bases in Newfoundland. Fort Pepperrell, at St. John's, is the Headquarters. This and the naval and air base at Argentia, and the air base at Stephenville, have all grown into thriving towns. The leases are now handled by the Dominion Government.

As in World War One, Newfoundlanders wrote another proud chapter in their long history in loyally responding to the Empire's call at the outbreak of World War Two. Their territory furnished vital defence bases. More than seven thousand men, a high percentage of all those of military age, participated in overseas service, including two artillery regiments and a night-fighter squadron of the Royal Air Force. In the Royal Navy and the Mercantile Marine, Newfoundlanders took part in many actions with the high seamanship of an island and fishing people. Women, also, served in many capacities. Shipbuilding was promoted and the Navy Dockyard at St. John's was considerably extended.

When this land of hills, lakes, rivers, and rocky sea-coast became Canada's tenth province, there was only one city, the capital, St. John's. It is beautifully situated, overlooking a vast and fine harbour where ships of many lands crowd the wharfs. Flights of stone steps lead up to the higher levels. Beyond the city streets lies Bowring Park, where bronze statues and memorials, the creation of men, enhance the natural beauty of the lovely wood- and water-fringed paths.